Sendero Luminoso and the Threat of Narcoterrorism

THE WASHINGTON PAPERS

. . . intended to meet the need for an authoritative, yet prompt, public appraisal of the major developments in world affairs.

President, CSIS: David M. Abshire

Series Editor: Walter Laqueur

Director of Publications: Nancy B. Eddy

Managing Editor: Donna R. Spitler

MANUSCRIPT SUBMISSION

The Washington Papers and Praeger Publishers welcome inquiries concerning manuscript submissions. Please include with your inquiry a curriculum vitae, synopsis, table of contents, and estimated manuscript length. Manuscripts must be between 120–200 double-spaced typed pages. All submissions will be peer reviewed. Submissions to *The Washington Papers* should be sent to *The Washington Papers*; The Center for Strategic and International Studies; 1800 K Street NW; Suite 400; Washington, DC 20006. Book proposals should be sent to Praeger Publishers; One Madison Avenue; New York NY 10010.

The Washington Papers/144

Sendero Luminoso and the Threat of Narcoterrorism

Gabriela Tarazona-Sevillano
with John B. Reuter

Foreword by David E. Long

Published with The Center for
Strategic and International Studies
Washington, D.C.

New York
Westport, Connecticut
London

Library of Congress Cataloging-in-Publication Data

Tarazona-Sevillano, Gabriela.
    Sendero Luminoso and the threat of narcoterrorism / Gabriela
Tarazona-Sevillano with John B. Reuter ; foreword by David Long.
        p.   cm. − (The Washington papers, ISSN 0278-937X ; 144)
    "Published with the Center for Strategic and International
Studies, Washington, D.C."
    Includes bibliographical references.
    ISBN 0-275-93642-2 (alk. paper). − ISBN 0-275-93643-0 (pbk. :
alk. paper)
        1. Sendero Luminoso (Guerilla group) 2. Terrorism−Peru. 3. Coca
industry−Peru. I. Reuter, John B. II. Center for Strategic and
International Studies (Washington, D.C.) III. Title. IV. Series.
HV6433.P4T37   1990
322.4′2′0985−dc20   90-37058

Library of Congress Catalog Card Number: 90-37058
ISBN: 0-275-93642-2 (cloth)
        0-275-93643-0 (paper)

First published in 1990

Praeger Publishers, One Madison Avenue, New York, NY 10010
An imprint of Greenwood Publishing Group, Inc.

Printed in the United States of America

The paper used in this book complies with the Permanent
Paper Standard issued by the National Information Standards
Organization (Z39.48-1984).

10   9   8   7   6   5   4   3   2   1

Contents

Foreword

There is the real possibility that the easing of cold war tensions will lead to the emergence of a multipolar world, upsetting the nuclear balance of terror achieved by the two superpowers. Despite all the global tensions of the post–World War II era, the fear of mutually assured destruction did place constraints on the level and degree of regional violence. The two superpowers would not tolerate the escalation of local or regional conflicts to the point where they threatened global peace. Without those constraints, one should expect that regional leaders and their opponents will be more tempted to solve their problems through armed violence.

The prospect of rising regional violence in the 1990s makes this study of a major South American terrorist group—Sendero Luminoso of Peru—particularly germane. Sendero's terrorist and guerrilla activities can serve as a blueprint of one type of violence that policy-makers will most likely be forced to deal with in the years ahead. If the focus of defense planning for the past 45 years on nuclear and large-scale conventional warfare is any indication, the West will be ill-prepared to deal with the kind of violence that Professor Tarazona-Sevillano has depicted.

Low-intensity conflict, which includes insurgencies, guerrilla warfare, and terrorism, has been particularly resistant to the dictates of global politics. The underlying causes of low-intensity conflict are generally local and regional in nature, even when universalist revolutionary doctrines such as communism and religious fundamentalism are used to justify acts of violence. Such conflicts are often either unrelated or only marginally related to global politics and thus have not been fundamentally affected by the thaw in global tensions.

Terrorism differs from other forms of low-intensity conflict in that it is primarily a psychological tactic. An act, no matter how violent or vile, is not terrorist unless someone is terrorized. The importance of public awareness to terrorism creates an anomaly for Western, particularly American, audiences, who often assume that if they have not heard of specific terrorist incidents, those incidents do not exist. In fact, thousands of people can be terrorized without Western audiences being aware of it. Western media coverage of terrorist acts is so uneven that most media audiences have a very incomplete understanding of the levels of terrorist activity and the geographical distribution of contemporary terrorist groups.

In the mid-1980s, for example, massive media coverage of such terrorist acts as the TWA flight 847 and *Achille Lauro* hijackings raised public awareness of Palestinian terrorist groups to the point where terrorism to many Americans is equated with the Middle East. At about the same time, Sendero Luminoso bombed a train near Cusco, Peru, killing and wounding a number of Americans. The U.S. government sent a medevac aircraft to transport the seriously wounded to the U.S. military hospital in Panama. Despite the brutality of the attack and the involvement of U.S. citizens, the incident barely made the back pages of the major U.S. daily papers.

It might come as a surprise to some that terrorist incidents in Latin America far exceed those in the Middle East, Northern Ireland, or, indeed, any other part of the world. And Sendero Luminoso is one of the most powerful and deadly terrorist groups anywhere. Its radical political doctrine is reminiscent of the Khmer Rouge, and with the recent disengagement of the Soviet Union, Senderistas are convinced that they have become the vanguard for world Communist revolution.

It is Sendero's links to the international drug trade, however, rather than its radical Maoist doctrine that make it a major source of concern to the United States. The symbiotic relationship that has grown up between drug traffickers and terrorists in Peru and neighboring Colombia in recent years has become a major, though relatively little known and understood, threat to the welfare of all Americans.

Professor Tarazona-Sevillano is supremely qualified to write about Sendero Luminoso. Trained as a lawyer in her native Peru, one of the few women so prepared, she was an assistant government prosecutor. Her intimate understanding of Peruvian society and politics and her objective, dispassionate analysis makes this an invaluable study for students of low-intensity conflict, the drug war, and Latin America, as well as for all Americans concerned about armed conflict in a changing international system.

David E. Long
U.S. Coast Guard Academy
June 1990

About the Author

Gabriela Tarazona-Sevillano served as a criminal affairs prosecutor of the Public Ministry in the judicial system of Peru from 1984 to 1986. Since 1986, she has been a visiting professor of international studies at Davidson College, Davidson, North Carolina. She was a visiting scholar at the Hoover Institution, Stanford University (summer 1989) and has served as a panelist for academic conferences on terrorism. Her articles have appeared in such publications as the *Atlanta Constitution* and the *Christian Science Monitor*. Gabriela Tarazona-Sevillano received her Bachelor of Law, political science, and J.D. degrees, as well as her Specialty Diploma in Juridic Corporate Science–International Commerce, from the Universidad Nacional de Trujillo in Trujillo, Peru.

Acknowledgments

This book would not have been possible without the assistance of friends and colleagues. I thank the staff of Davidson College for providing me with initial support — especially John P. Brockway for his constant help and Jack Perry for his precise and keen counsel in delicate matters. I also owe special thanks to David Long and Robert Jones for their wise advice and support during this project and to John Reuter and Wes Hofferbert for their assistance in preparing the manuscript.

I thank my father in Peru — Dr. Pedro R. Tarazona — as well as friends in the Peruvian judicial system who provided invaluable assistance. And I am grateful to Ana Maria Bromley, Superior Criminal Affairs judge, Court of El Callao; Juan Malca Pérez, attorney at the Lima Prosecutor's office; officials in the Ministry of Interior who granted access to unpublished data in the development of the Sendero phenomenon; and my sister Ethel for her valuable research assistance in Peru.

This manuscript has been made possible by a fellowship grant from the Earhart Foundation of Ann Arbor, Michigan, and by a faculty research grant from Davidson College.

Finally, my appreciation goes to my husband Aldo for his help, care, and encouragement during the realization of this project.

All errors of interpretation are mine alone.

Summary

Sendero Luminoso — the "Shining Path" — ranks among the most elusive, secretive, and brutal guerrilla organizations in the world. For a decade, it has carried out a violent, clandestine rebellion in Peru unlike any seen thus far in the Western Hemisphere. Strengthened by adherence to the theories of Karl Marx, Vladimir Lenin, and Mao Zedong, the insurgency is determined to overthrow Peru's existing socioeconomic system and restructure the state with its own unique interpretation of communism.

The Sendero Luminoso movement first emerged in May 1980, at the time when democracy returned to Peru after 12 years of military dictatorship. Since then it has continued to grow steadily. Once a radical uprising limited to the Andean highlands of Ayacucho, it is now a movement of national proportions that has woven itself into the fabric of Peruvian society. At first essentially ignored as a temporary disturbance, it is recognized today as the Peruvian government's greatest domestic problem. Even the nation's hyperinflation pales in comparison.

Unlike many other terrorist groups, Sendero Luminoso is founded upon an intellectual infrastructure. The movement is led by the now legendary Abimael Guzmán, a former philosophy professor revered by Senderistas as "the fourth sword of communism" (after Marx, Lenin, and Mao). Following Guzmán are university students, graduates, and others well educated in the arts and sciences. These individuals form a far-reaching support network that provides the organization with valuable information and services – medical, legal, technological, and psychological. Their presence ensures that the insurrection cannot be easily wiped from the Peruvian slate.

The body of the movement, however, is drawn from Peru's long-neglected Indian and mestizo populations. By exacerbating class consciousness and social resentment among these people, Sendero leaders have shrewdly turned a critical national situation to their own advantage. Feelings of hatred and revenge have risen from exploitation to fuel the insurrection, resulting in acts of intense violence and destruction. Peru's already fragile democracy is further weakened, as the rural and urban underclasses become attached to Sendero ideologically and emotionally.

The government's dilemma is complicated by the emergence of "narcoterrorism," a mutually beneficial relationship that has arisen between the cocaine syndicate and Sendero Luminoso. These two organizations have different objectives and ideologies, but share a mutual enemy – the Peruvian government and its armed services. Hence they have combined forces to form a powerful and destructive alliance, a partnership that greatly increases the existing threat to Peru's democratic system and U.S. interests in the region.

The impact of the Sendero Luminoso on Peruvian society should not be underestimated; it is a desperate and expensive burden for a new democratic government already besieged by complex and far-reaching problems. Since the armed struggle began in 1980, Sendero has not once yielded the initiative; nor has either of the two administrations elected in that period been able to counter the insurrection effectively. Both politicians and army officers now openly admit the war is clearly being lost. If U.S. and Western diplomats and policymakers are to assist, they must first understand the peculiar and very personal nature of Peru's affliction as well as its possible international repercussions.

1

Historical Background

José Carlos Mariátegui, a Lima journalist, founded the Socialist Party of Peru (Partido Socialista del Perú or PSP) in 1928 with the conviction that the only way to achieve power and change the structure of Peru's economically polarized society was through armed struggle. Mariátegui died just two years later, and his party, under the direction of Eudocio Ravines, joined the Communist International movement (the Comintern) and was redefined as the Communist Party of Peru (Partido Comunista del Perú or PCP). From that time, the party continued to grow steadily as the only Marxist political organization in Peru until the early 1960s. Then, because of significant developments in the global Communist movement (the Cuban Revolution, the Sino-Soviet split, Nikita Khrushchev's denunciation of Joseph Stalin) and as a result of internal controversies, the party slowly began to splinter. By 1975, the Peruvian Left had splintered into some 20 different political organizations.[1]

One of the earliest, yet most fundamental, of the party's fissures occurred in 1964 at the Fourth National Party Conference. At this time the PCP's two principal ideological factions, pro-Soviet and pro-Maoist, culminated a long-simmering ideological dispute by splitting the party into two

1

separate blocs. Although agreeing that Peru was destined for Communist rule, the two camps differed on the methods by which this state should be achieved. The Soviet cluster proposed a peaceful transition based on reform; the Maoists, in contrast, insisted that the only way to unseat the landed and bourgeois classes was through armed struggle—the "extended or protracted war" of which Mao had written years before.

After breaking with the Soviet-oriented sector of the party, those leaning toward a Maoist doctrine reassembled and called themselves the Communist Party of Peru—Red Flag (PCP—Bandera Roja or PCP-BR). The 1964 schism did not end the internal quarreling, however. After the second meeting of the new PCP Central Committee in 1970, another major, irreparable split took place. Abimael Guzmán, the Central Committee plenum president, took charge of a new faction named the Communist Party of Peru—By Way of the Shining Path of Mariátegui (PCP—por el Sendero Luminoso de Mariátegui or PCP-SL). The new party was established with the belief that the conditions necessary for radical revolution were already present in Peru; the potential only needed to be unleashed. (The remainder of the Maoist camp, led by Saturnino Paredes, retained the name "Red Flag" and believed that further preparation for revolution was necessary.)

Thus Sendero Luminoso was born, a political party that would radically affect the future of Peru without ever fielding an electoral candidate.

Abimael Guzmán: Founder of the Insurgency

On December 4, 1934, Abimael Guzmán was born out of wedlock to Berenice Reynoso and Abismael Guzmán Silva in Tambo, Arequipa. He received his primary and secondary education at La Salle, a private Catholic school in Arequipa attended mainly by the children of affluent townspeople. Guzmán is remembered by teachers and classmates as an unusually dedicated student. His interest in politics may be traced to La Salle, where he and several friends founded a group to study all political theories. Arequipa was rife with political turmoil during this period (the early 1950s), and the group observed with interest as local citizens struggled for their rights. Guzmán would later comment that the Arequipa experience had taught him that true change could only be brought about through violence.

After graduating from La Salle, Guzmán entered the University of San Agustín de Arequipa. There he wrote a law thesis, "About the Democratic Bourgeois State," as well as a philosophy thesis, "Regarding Kant's Theory of Space." Initially a Social Democrat, Guzmán grew increasingly cynical about the parliamentary path to socialism as his university career progressed; by graduation, he had become a committed Marxist-Leninist. He remained at the University of San Agustín to teach after graduation, but was soon hired away by the University of San Cristóbal de Huamanga (UNSCH) in Ayacucho.

The move to Ayacucho in 1962 proved to be of great importance in Guzmán's continuing intellectual development. There he became more aware of the true poverty in which most Peruvians live and the corresponding political implications. Interest in the peasant masses led Guzmán to study the writings of Mao Zedong, and these studies, in turn, served as the impetus for trips to China in 1965 and 1967. These trips were clearly a watershed in his political thinking: he came away fully convinced that his country must follow a Marxist-Leninist-Maoist path to development — similar to China's — if genuine social change were to be achieved. Back in Ayacucho, Guzmán devoted himself to the study of Mariátegui. He drew clear parallels between the writings of Peru's original socialist commentator and Mao, thereby discovering that Mao's model for revolution harmonized well with Mariátegui's description of Peru's unbalanced social structure. With this hypothesis in mind, Guzmán broke from the PCP-BR in 1970 to form Sendero Luminoso. Interestingly, he insisted that he was not forming a new organization, but rather returning the party formed by Mariátegui to its founder's original intentions.

Guzmán has not been seen in public since 1979, which was just before Sendero's armed struggle began. Many speculate that he is dead. In July 1988, the extreme leftist newspaper *El Diario*, in an entire issue dedicated to Sendero Luminoso, featured a personal interview with Guzmán. The veracity of this report, billed as the "interview of the century," has been widely accepted.[2] Yet, the question of Guzmán's mortality has enhanced his mythical status within the insurgency and throughout the nation.

The Birth of Sendero Luminoso

The Sendero Luminoso movement was founded in early 1970 in Ayacucho, a highland department in the southwestern Peruvian Andes. Ayacucho is home to more than 500,000 people. Because of its geographical isolation, it has been perennially neglected by successive Peruvian administrations, both military and democratic. As a result, the department has the country's lowest income per capita and the lowest share of the gross national product (GNP). It also has Peru's highest number of inhabitants without potable water (66.96 percent), electricity (82.86 percent), and sewage removal (90.67 percent). Only Apurímac, a neighboring department, has a higher illiteracy rate (45 percent of the population).[3] Deprivation of this magnitude makes the department, as well as the surrounding region, an ideal breeding ground for a Maoist-type insurrection. Sendero leaders shrewdly seized upon this fact as they planted the seeds of their movement.

Within Ayacucho, the Sendero movement was based at UNSCH. Founded by the Spanish in 1677, this institution was intended to serve as a regional education center—a goal that in recent years has assumed an ironic twist.[4] These intentions were reemphasized in 1959 when, after 80 years of dormancy, the university was reopened by President

Manuel Prado. In response to the tremendous need in Ayacucho, the UNSCH was to concentrate on educational programs specifically to help the Indian and mestizo inhabitants of the department improve their standard of living. Hence, the curriculum was composed primarily of agricultural and educational training and other practical programs of study.

From the moment it reopened, the university became the center of cultural life in the area, its programs permeated with the energy of the many young faculty members. These professors, along with the numerous foreign scholars who had come to UNSCH through international exchange programs, injected a new social conscience into the populace, enhancing Ayacucho's regional status as an educational epicenter. The region further benefited from a university-sponsored service called "Social Projection," through which professors and students provided educational and practical instruction for members of the surrounding communities. This locally popular university, when combined with a desperately poor regional population, provided an excellent starting point for a Maoist-style insurrection.

Abimael Guzmán joined the university faculty in 1962 as a professor of philosophy and social science in the Education Department. Already a member of the PCP when he arrived in Ayacucho, he immediately joined the local chapter and began to use his teaching position to disseminate Communist theory. His charisma both in and out of the classroom, his magnetic personality, his obviously deep conviction, and his persuasive arguments soon attracted many followers — students, local inhabitants, and other faculty members.

In 1963, just one year after his arrival, Guzmán was elected to the university's executive council, the body responsible for directing all institutional policy at UNSCH. In addition to his council membership, Guzmán served as a director of the General Studies program, a two-year series of courses obligatory for all incoming students.[5] By combining his administrative clout and dynamic teaching abilities, Guzmán was continually able to increase the large pool of students that identified with the Marxist-Maoist doctrine. Student organizations within the university began to take on a definite Maoist tint. From these groups, Guzmán drew the most devoted and promising members, entrusting them with additional responsibilities in his evolving political party. In 1970, he was appointed director of personnel (faculty and staff) at the university and used this position to dismiss his political opponents, replacing them with others closer to his beliefs. Thus Guzmán profoundly influenced the faculty, the student body, and the local community.

Expansion of the Movement

Within the university, the Education Department most effectively dispersed Sendero dogma. This department — the largest of the university's 12 formal programs of study — accounted for some 42.5 percent of the entire student body, the vast majority of whom came to study at Huamanga from the rural departments of Huancavelica, Apurímac, and, of course, Ayacucho. Because many of these students intended to return to their original communities to teach, the department provided an ideal setting for Guzmán and his ideological soul mates to amplify their list of followers. Students became attracted to the persuasive Marxist-Leninist-Maoist doctrine and, upon graduation, soon became indoctrinators themselves. After returning to their homelands, they taught the Sendero line to younger generations. Because these young teachers were often the only educated members of their communities, they were greatly respected, and their explanations of political and economic theory were generally accepted without question.

An organization already in existence, the Student Revolutionary Front (Frente Estudiantil Revolucionario or FER), provided Sendero with a national network to spread its doctrine. The FER took shape during a period in which unusually high levels of Marxism and dialectical logic were being taught in the Peruvian university system – a result of curriculum reforms implemented under the administration of Juan Velasco Alvarado (1968–1975). Peruvian students previously unversed in the intricacies of socialism became familiar with, and in many cases captivated with, the concepts of dialectical and historical materialism. Many concluded that the only way to lessen the polarities in the standard of living between Peru's upper and lower classes was through communism. During the early 1970s, the entire FER, which was based in Lima, began to adopt Guzmán's ideology as its own. By 1976, FER publications were virtually indistinguishable from those published by Guzmán and his followers at the University of San Cristóbal. Well-trained "cells" of FER students began to visit university campuses throughout Peru to heighten the political awareness of the student population and promote the class struggle. This strategy proved effective on both rural and urban campuses, where students of Indian and mestizo ancestry were able to identify personally with or relate to the Sendero doctrine as it was presented to them. Sizable numbers of sympathizers were recruited quickly at almost every public university in Peru.[6]

It might seem that the Sendero Luminoso movement could be viewed as "petit bourgeois" liberalism if the university circles where it was founded are considered alone. In truth, however, the movement has much deeper roots among the entire Peruvian substratum. As scholars David Scott Palmer and Cynthia McClintock have documented in detail, the Sendero doctrine was well disseminated among the rural inhabitants of Ayacucho, Apurímac, and Huancavelica.[7] Later, in urban areas, much support was garnered from the constantly expanding shantytowns that ring Peru's metropolitan areas.

Roughly 40 percent of Peru's potential labor force is employed under stable conditions. Although the actual unemployment figure is relatively low (8.2 percent), 51.4 percent of the eligible work force remains underemployed (see figure 1).[8] A 1986 study by Peru's National Institute of

FIGURE 1
Eligible Labor Force of Peru, 1986

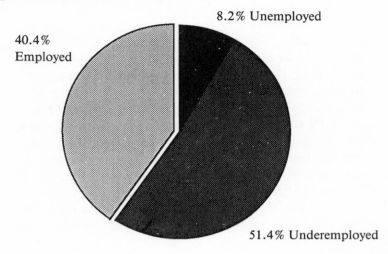

Source: Data from Instituto Nacional de Estadística, *Compendio Estadístico*, May 1988.

Statistics revealed that the majority of Peru's population is not integrated into the country's economic system and does not benefit from the services that the state theoretically furnishes to its citizens and taxpayers.[9] Millions of informally employed Peruvians pay no taxes and make no contribution to the official economy of Peru. They must struggle to meet their immediate day-to-day needs through temporary employment. It is this struggling population mass that Sendero has targeted, and it is from this sector that most of the movement's adherents have been drawn.

This socioeconomic exclusion has far greater effects than fundamental economic hardship. Peruvian scholars postulate that the perceived unjust social structure, in which many are deprived of the most basic economic necessities, leads the downtrodden to conclude that they are being victimized by an unknown, aggressive entity—an abstract interpretation of a very real situation.[10] These feelings of economic oppression are complicated and augmented by feelings of cultural strangulation inherited from the Spanish-imposed culture of some five centuries earlier. This legacy of cultural and economic oppression persists today as Peru, like many other Latin American countries, struggles to keep pace economically and technologically with the rest of the Western world. Yet no obvious enemy exists toward which these conflicts and the resulting feelings of intense angst and resentment may be directed. These emotions are therefore turned inward toward Peruvian society, leading to internal violence and strife. Peruvians who have studied the phenomenon label it "structural violence" (*violencia estructural*).[11]

Into this volatile situation comes Sendero Luminoso, portraying itself as the one able to understand and solve the problems that have plagued rural and urban underclass Peruvians for centuries. Cleverly denouncing the government and congress (including the parliamentary Left) for their wickedness, Sendero Luminoso proposes to destroy these oppressive structures represented by the state.

2

Ideology and Goals

Mariátegui: Father of the Peruvian Left

José Carlos Mariátegui is generally considered the father of the Peruvian Left. Almost all of Peru's Marxist parties refer to Mariátegui as their inspiration, with each espousing its own unique interpretation of his writings—interpretations that in many cases differ widely. His magnum opus, *Seven Interpretive Essays on Peruvian Reality*, is a Marxist evaluation of Peru's socioeconomic situation.[1] The leadership of the Sendero Luminoso movement has drawn its characterization of Peruvian reality almost directly from this work. A brief survey of Mariátegui and his life will clarify the perspective from which Peru's most significant social, political, and economic analysis was written.

Mariátegui was born into a mestizo family of modest means in 1895.[2] His mother was a seamstress, his father a state employee. The family situation was less than ideal: Mariátegui's father abandoned the marriage at an early stage, a loss the future writer never fully understood and one that troubled him deeply his entire life. His mother, who was extremely poor, was left to raise José Carlos and two siblings on her own. Mariátegui's left leg was crippled in a playground accident at age eight. Always an unhealthy child, he was ultimately confined to bed for two years because of this injury. During his extended convalescence, Mariátegui first became interested in books. He would become a voracious reader by the time he recovered.

In 1909, at age 14, he took a job as a "copyboy" for Lima's *La Prensa* newspaper, and within a few years, he rose to the rank of reporter. The young writer's position at the newspaper gave him access to the highly politicized Peruvian intelligentsia—writers, politicians, and other reporters. Conversing with these men, Mariátegui found himself increasingly interested in politics and political theory, especially as related to his native Peru. It was, in fact, his political writing that eventually led him to be hired by another Lima newspaper, *El Tiempo*. Given considerable editorial freedom there, Mariátegui's critiques of the Peruvian government became increasingly acrimonious, reflecting the social and economic crisis that consumed Lima between 1917 and 1919. About this time, Mariátegui began to refer to himself as a socialist.

When his leftist editorials became too strongly slanted for *El Tiempo*, Mariátegui departed to found a socialist, working-class newspaper called *La Razón*. His new publication was dedicated, as the masthead declared, "to one principle: the truth."[3] Much of *La Razón* was devoted to the developments of the Communist movement in Europe, subject matter other Lima newspapers had not previously broached. This paper achieved a relatively successful reputation in the city until 1919, when, after a period of particularly critical editorials about the government, President Augusto B. Leguia shut down the operation and "suggested" that Mariátegui and his fellow reporter César Falcón take a "sabbatical" in Europe, which they did.

Although he was in effect being exiled, Mariátegui was nonetheless excited about the prospect of visiting Europe; it was a firsthand opportunity to meet and talk with the socialist and Communist radicals he had been reading and writing about for years. In Paris, he was befriended by Henri Barbusse, cofounder of the French Communist Party, and the *Clarté* intellectuals, who further spurred his interest in Marxism. The Marxist *Clarté* group was also responsible for introducing Mariátegui to the "psychological dimension of the struggle toward gaining revolutionary awareness."[4] From Paris, Mariátegui traveled to Rome, where he followed with interest the fall of Gabriele D'Annunzio's socialist rule and the rise of fascism. Also while in Rome, under the tutelage of Pierro Gobetti, he crystallized his vision of the world's "tainted history" of feudalism, capitalism, and imperialism.[5] Before returning to Peru, Mariátegui also journeyed to Germany, where he observed the then-powerful Social Democratic Party split into two rival factions – the Leninist Communists and the Orthodox Socialists. The writer became persuaded by Lenin's argument that the parliamentary path to socialism was ineffectual and that only through revolution spearheaded by a "conscious vanguard" could a nation be launched on a political path leading to communism. Later, in Lima, he would write that the trip was a "revelation whereby he suddenly began to know truly the country in which he had previously lived almost like a stranger."[6]

Mariátegui returned to Peru in March 1923, profoundly committed to the idea of creating and nourishing a Leninist-bent socialist movement there. Upon arrival, he immediately reestablished himself as a socialist intellectual and launched a series of lectures and editorials designed to inform and educate the public in concepts of world historical reform. Most Peruvian workers and students had not yet been exposed to Marxism and the Leninist concept of global revolution.[7] Mariátegui encouraged his audiences to consider the possibility and even necessity of anticolonial revolution in countries such as Peru, following to a certain degree the pattern of socialist reform that had already begun in Europe. The writer was instilling among the populace a radical interpretation of Peru's national situation.

Besides founding the Socialist Party of Peru, Mariátegui is best known for his transcendental analysis of the Peruvian situation and major literary work – *Seven Inter-*

pretive Essays on Peruvian Reality.[8] First published in 1928, this work is fundamentally a historical assessment of the socioeconomic situation in Peru since the preconquest period. In the essays, Mariátegui interprets Peruvian circumstances from a Marxist-Leninist point of view, explaining at great length the development of class separations and the resulting imbalance of power. The issues he discusses were not new to Peruvian society, but they were controversial; because Mariátegui was the first to apply a Marxist analysis, his work provoked considerable uproar. Of the collection, three essays in particular—"Outline of the Economic Evolution," "The Problem of Land," and "The Problem of the Indian"—would later highly influence the Sendero Luminoso characterization of the Peruvian situation.[9]

In a synoptic discussion of Mariátegui's importance in the development of revolutionary thought in Peru, John M. Baines presents Mariátegui as a man who wanted to unite the opposite fragments of his identity, a man who typified the struggle of his generation. "As a mestizo," Baines writes, "[Mariátegui] was caught between Peru's two mutually antagonistic worlds—the Indian and the white European. He was a product of these two cultures, yet not wholly a part of either."[10] The writer also failed to gain the full social acceptance either of his fellow intellectuals or of the ordinary people whose cause he championed. As an unlettered, self-educated, struggling journalist, Mariátegui was always on the periphery of the circle of educated intellectuals in Lima who frequently sojourned in Paris and Rome. As a well-read, perceptive, and somewhat aloof individual, he was not accepted as an equal by the man-on-the-street. His life and writings may be viewed as a struggle to replace his alienation (and, by extension, that of others) with acceptance. In this light Baines casts Mariátegui in the role of "the spokesman": "The spokesman is he who defines new identities for changing persons, reshapes old expectations and formulates new demands to fit their lifeways."[11]

Mariátegui's writings devote much attention to the

necessity of fueling a sense of nationalism within the Peruvian populace. Along these lines, he was especially concerned with bringing justice to those he considered the true Peruvians—the Indians and the mestizos. These two racial types have historically suffered from prejudice in Peru and throughout the rest of Latin America. Mariátegui deeply resented the societal prejudice and refused to believe that the Spanish and their descendants were racially superior. Rejecting his own Spanish heritage, the writer idealized the Indian race and its legacy. He reasoned that true equality for the masses could be achieved if Peru adopted a thoroughly socialist society—one that fully incorporated the Indians and mestizos. To accomplish this goal, Mariátegui proposed new recognition of the Incas' notable accomplishments and a modern restoration of their socioeconomic system.

In Mariátegui's eyes, the great Inca Empire Twantinsuyo (c. 1200–1532) was so structured that its subjects were not only cared for materially but also were raised with a sense of purpose—an identity in life and a loyalty to the state. He concedes that Inca rule was theocratic and despotic, but justifies these properties as characteristic of all regimes of antiquity. In the spirit of Manuel Gonzales Prada, one of the first Peruvian authors to enhance the reign of the Incas, Mariátegui depicts the Inca period with great nostalgia. He paints a glowing portrait of an ideal society in which all prospered.

The economy that supported the Inca Empire was primarily agrarian. The functional socioeconomic unit of the system was the *ayllu*, a type of family cooperative that actually predated Inca rule. Land surrounding Inca villages was divided into these family-worked, nontransferable lots; pasture, woodlands, and water were shared by all in the township federations, as were the public works of Twantinsuyo. In addition to an impressive network of roads throughout the empire, the Incas devised a complex irrigational canal system and agricultural terraces (*andenes*) that allowed farming on the steep Andean slopes. These accomplishments attest to the degree of economic and social organization reached by the Incas, wrote Mariátegui, and "cannot be negated or disparaged for having developed under an autocratic regime."[12] The collectivist nature of the economic structure was bolstered by the Incas' religious beliefs, which included strong emphasis on social duty that supposedly subdued individualistic tendencies. The combined religious, economic, and social systems, Mariátegui attests, amounted to "Inca Communism."[13]

The fifteenth-century Spanish conquest interrupted this "ideal" state. The conquest, as is well documented, was a military and ecclesiastical enterprise, based largely on greed and exploitation.[14] Although the Spanish did succeed in extracting phenomenal quantities of precious metals from Peru and in partially converting thousands of Indians to Catholicism, they were unable to replace the Incan system with one of equal or greater efficiency. Instead, they brought to the New World Spain's crumbling social institutions — among them, feudalism.[15] The effects of Spanish rule were catastrophic for Peru: The Indians were enslaved, the agrarian economy was abandoned for mining, and the centuries-old Incan religion was undermined. Except for a few small pockets scattered in the isolated highlands, Peruvian society basically disintegrated.

When Peru eventually gained its independence from Spain, Mariátegui continues, it was merely political independence. The rule of Lima had replaced the rule of Madrid, but the exploitation of many at the hands of few continued. The war was fought by *criollos*, descendants of the Spanish who sought to rule Peru without European intervention. Their elitist scheme would never entail the restructuring of Peru's political and economic system to allow full participation by the Indians and the mestizos. Therefore, Mariátegui concluded that Peru's distorted development under the Spanish and their descendants had wrought an "alien" socioeconomic system imposed upon the populace by force.

Analyzing the first century of Peru's independence, Mariátegui wrote that the perpetuation of feudalism in

Peru — what he referred to as *gamonalismo* — should be viewed as the continuation not only of a medieval economic system but also of a warped and tenacious social philosophy.[16] The *haciendas*, or large estates, that dominated the rural economy were sustained by the exploitation of Indian and mestizo laborers. The *hacendado*, or landowner, whom Mariátegui called the *gamonal*, did not differ substantially from a feudal lord in his exercise of immense power and absolute control over land and people alike. Moreover, the coastal haciendas, among the largest in the nation, were supported with substantial infusions of foreign capital, ensuring that their production would focus on such export crops as sugar and cotton. As a result, the cultivation of foodstuffs for the Peruvian market was neglected, and food was increasingly imported to meet domestic needs. Thus, the Peruvian state wore the trappings of political independence, while the masses remained within the grip of imperialism.

The hacienda system also damaged Peru by stifling the development of a market economy. The haciendas were virtually self-sufficient, greatly impeding the evolution of capitalism that had taken place in post-feudal Europe. Only in Lima did true capitalism begin to evolve, largely because of the presence of British and, later, U.S. banks that loaned money to entrepreneurial nationals. As Peru's debt to foreigners continued to climb, Mariátegui claimed that the Peruvian bourgeoisie had "sold out," putting the nation in the hands of outsiders and plunging Peru deeper into the grave of economic colonialism. Peru was thus ruled by the interests of the landed aristocracy, mainly of Spanish descent, and the urban bourgeoisie. The Indians and mestizos, however, remained outsiders in their own country.

Mariátegui proposed a revolution to change this state of affairs, after which the nation could be rebuilt on its indigenous, preconquest cultural and economic heritage. Realizing that it would be necessary to awaken the masses and establish a new nationalistic pride and ideology if this goal were to be accomplished, Mariátegui took on the task of writing and publishing his essays, all of which promoted change through revolutionary Marxism-Leninism. Applying what he had learned from Gobetti and the Italians, he wrote that once the economic structure had been altered, other societal changes would follow. Foremost among them would be the condition of the Indians. Given an economic footing, he reasoned, they would inevitably improve their social situation. From Mariátegui's point of view, the Indian situation was a question of economics, not morals.

The new state would combine, then, the elements of the Inca Empire's societal structure with a modern socialist economic system.[17] Mariátegui theorized that, by combining the preconquest communism with a modern strain of socialism, a new socioeconomic structure would be born. In the proposed system, each Peruvian would have a sense of his rights and responsibilities rooted firmly in the nation's economy. The new state would build upon the heritage of the Incas—an organized, disciplined, hardworking society—not upon the Spanish model; it would thus reflect Peru's precolonial history and traditions. And the reinstatement of these traditions would ultimately unite the Peruvian nation.

Mariátegui died in 1929 at age 35. Given his youth and physical disability, his accomplishments are decidedly impressive. It is perhaps more impressive, however, that his ideas for a new Peruvian state did not die with him. They would be reborn some 40 years later as the theoretical base for Sendero Luminoso.

The Spiritual Leadership of Abimael Guzmán

Abimael Guzmán drew Mariátegui's philosophy into the working doctrine of Sendero Luminoso by synthesizing the thought of Marx, Lenin, Mao, and Mariátegui. His new doctrine was designed specifically for Peru's rural and urban underclasses, the Indians and mestizos about whom Mariátegui had been so concerned. As the ideology spread,

Guzmán began to assume a semimythical stature. Today he is known throughout Peru by his *nom de guerre*, or pseudonym — "Presidente Gonzalo, the fourth sword of Marxism."

Guzmán's ideology is extracted from the writings of the greatest thinkers of the Communist pantheon. While still a university student, he began to characterize the Peruvian situation in terms of Marxist political philosophy. In Guzmán's mind, the Peruvian state exemplified the evils of colonialism and feudalism. He believed that the rural and urban underclasses, by far the greatest sector of the populace, were grossly exploited by those owning the means of production, the smallest sector of the populace. The inequity of the situation was magnified because those benefiting most from the labor of the marginalized masses were almost entirely of Spanish, rather than "true" Peruvian, descent. Like Marx, Guzmán thought the time had come for the masses to rise up as a revolutionary class, to conquer the existing state and take power for themselves. Only then would real emancipation take place.

Guzmán built intellectually upon his Marxist base by studying the writings of Lenin, works that proved early and significant influences on him. Just as Lenin changed the name of his party to "Communist" in 1917 to differentiate it from social democratic strains of Marxism, so too did Guzmán. In the late 1950s, Guzmán ceased referring to himself as a Social Democrat and devoted himself to the Communist cause. When asked about this change, he deferred to Lenin: Meaningful change, he explained, would never be accomplished through the peaceful transition the Social Democrats advocated; only revolution, such as that of the Bolsheviks or Mao Zedong, could usher in the beginning of a new era. While studying Lenin, Guzmán became more intensely radical, deepening his convictions that genuine class struggle must precede true reform.[18] He has also exhibited an unabashed admiration for the life and ideas of Joseph Stalin, a revelation that may explain his ruthless advocacy of unfettered violence in the revolutionary process.[19]

It was Mao Zedong, however, who ultimately had the greatest influence on Guzmán. The Peruvian saw important similarities between his country and prerevolutionary China: Both were semicolonial and semifeudal, both had large rural populations, and both were experiencing trauma as they undertook industrialization. Mao's ideology and strategy of taking power through a "protracted march" captivated Guzmán, who reasoned that a similar approach might be successful in Peru. Just a few years later, Guzmán's guidelines for bringing Sendero Luminoso to power in Peru would rely heavily on the writings of Mao. Two concepts to which Guzmán devoted special attention can be traced to the Chinese Communist: First, the idea that the revolution must be born in the countryside – a peasant war – building up a stronghold from which to take the urban areas; and, second, the goal for which the war is being fought, a "New Democratic Republic." Sendero Luminoso's military strategy is also based largely on Mao's, with Guzmán emphasizing that a government army can indeed be defeated by a much smaller and less-well-equipped force if campaigns are planned meticulously and the militants are motivated ideologically.

Finally, Guzmán's impetus for initiating the movement can be traced, as Guzmán has stated repeatedly, to José Carlos Mariátegui and his *Seven Interpretive Essays on Peruvian Reality.* "These essays," Baines points out in his excellent study of Mariátegui and Peruvian revolution, "read like the writings of a dispossessed, rootless man attempting to create the feeling of racial, spiritual, and cultural unity for other dispossessed and rootless men."[20] Guzmán, also a mestizo with an irregular family background, must share these feelings and the hostility that accompanies them. Casting himself in the role of Mariátegui's ideological heir, he decided to carry out the revolution the writer had envisioned some 40 years before. It became his goal to unite the marginal classes in a violent, vindictive revolt that would destroy Eurocentric Peru and build a new nation grounded in indigenous institutions. In the process, the Indians and mestizos – the genuine Peruvians – would be redeemed.[21]

Assuming the post of spiritual and ideological father to the Sendero Luminoso movement has given Guzmán an almost messianic stature in the eyes of thousands of followers. His doctrine pretends to impose a hopeful order over the chaos of Peru's economic, social, and political plights, offering a bright new path toward the future. Guzmán and the movement he leads attempt to appear as liberators to the millions of destitute Peruvians shackled by centuries of poverty and mistreatment.

To his disciples, President Gonzalo is "the most important Marxist-Leninist alive today."[22] He has been dubbed "the fourth sword of Marxism" after Marx himself, and Lenin and Mao, in appreciation of his contributions to Marxist ideology and his commitment to the fight against global revisionism and the imperialistic hegemony of the Soviets and Chinese (whom Sendero claims have "betrayed" the revolution). Senderistas claim two major philosophical contributions for Guzmán: A synthesis of the laws of dialectics into one – the law of contradiction – and the discovery and formulation of the five phases of the armed struggle (see chapter 3). Guzmán is also responsible for conceiving a plan that will theoretically prevent in postrevolutionary Peru the endorsement of capitalism that Sendero alleges has occurred in the Soviet Union and China.

The prospect of fighting a revolution only to have its outcome mollified by revisionist policymakers is disparaging to members of Sendero Luminoso, and Guzmán receives much praise within the movement for his strong stance against the possibility of such a scenario. Guzmán is perceived by his followers as wielding a heavenly blade against the three principal revisionists: the Russians (Khrushchev, Brezhnev, and Gorbachev); the "roach," Deng Xiaoping; and the "political dwarf," Enver Hoxa. He has inaugurated a new stage in the history of Marxism, the fourth: Gonzalism.[23] On this much grander scale, those associated with

Sendero consider Gonzalo and his theory the vanguard of global communism, "the beacon of world revolution."[24]

Senderistas highly praise Guzmán's conception of Bureaucratic Capitalism, which the Sendero leader explains as a late form of capitalism born out of feudalism (the landed classes became the new bourgeoisie in the form of bankers and monopolistic merchants) under imperialist domination and monopolistic exploitation. This form of capitalism aligns itself with the power of the state and uses the state's financial and bureaucratic means as an economic lever. This phenomenon generates a new faction – the bureaucratic bourgeoisie. Now, says Guzmán, Peru harbors a form of capitalism that was originally monopolistic and has become state-operated. Guzmán proclaims that his thesis makes it possible to understand the Peruvian situation in light of the coexistence of semi-feudalistic land tenure (he classifies as semi-feudalistic the cooperatives resulting from the agrarian reform), Bureaucratic Capitalism, and imperialist domination, principally that of the United States.

According to Abimael Guzmán, the beginning of the popular war in 1980 devastatingly reveals the crisis of Bureaucratic Capitalism. Guzmán claims that the collapse of the present system is under way, that the viability of capitalism is historically terminated, and that the task of Sendero is to bury it. Bureaucratic Capitalism has entered a state of complete crisis that will only worsen. Guzmán claims that this form of capitalism was impaired from the moment of birth, because "feudalism is decrepit and imperialism is agonizing."[25]

Abimael Guzmán has not been seen in public since the Sendero Luminoso movement went underground in 1979, and there is much controversy as to whether he is dead or alive. Whether planned or accidental, the resulting aura of mystery around Guzmán has led some to credit him with almost superhuman powers. Captured Senderistas report that he is alive and well, directing the revolution from a hidden lair where he is guarded by the insurgency's toughest militants – men who are "red, body and soul" – and equipped with the most modern weapons available.[26]

Evidence that Guzmán is still alive and at the helm of Sendero surfaced in 1988. According to Luis Arce Borja, chief editor of the leftist *El Diario* newspaper, he and his information manager were granted a lengthy interview with Guzmán in July 1988. Arce states that Guzmán requested an interview with *El Diario* to publicize the achievements of the movement's first national congress. Some Peruvian intellectuals, however, believe that Guzmán staged this interview to affirm that the insurgency and its leadership continue to thrive despite the capture of Osmán Morote, Sendero's reputed second-in-command. Although the alleged interview was conducted at Guzmán's secret headquarters, Arce and his assistant were blindfolded during their journey to this heavily guarded locale and could not guess at Guzmán's whereabouts. Arce's purported interview is given credence by its breadth of knowledge on both the ideological underpinnings and future goals of Sendero Luminoso. The interview apparently proved sufficiently convincing to officials in the Peruvian government, who seized all printed copies of the document, suspended further production, and temporarily detained Arce for interrogation.

Even top-level Senderistas in custody have been unable to reveal Guzmán's whereabouts. He will surface, they say, when the movement triumphs, at which time he will walk in the streets, a savior and leader of the people. To those attached to Sendero, Guzmán is more than an ideological leader: he is the guiding light, the father of a new age in Peru. The ethereal nature of his character is portrayed in Sendero propaganda. On posters, pamphlets, and wall paintings, he is depicted as a bright, soaring flame, burning with ideological passion and power.[27] In contrast, Marx, Lenin, and Mao, who appear with him, are shown in the traditional head-and-shoulders format. To Peruvians disillusioned with the seeming inadequacies of their elected officials, this vision of a genuinely effectual leader is indeed appealing.

There is little question that Guzmán has built his own cult of personality. Gordon H. McCormick, drawing from a number of sources, defines four basic elements of such a characterization:

> (1) the group leader, in this case Abimael Guzmán, is believed to possess a unique vision and superhuman qualities; (2) group followers unquestionably accept the leader's views, statements, and judgements [sic]; (3) they comply with his orders and directives without condition; and (4) they give the leader unqualified support and devotion.[28]

Such a relationship, when functional, creates a spiritual fusion between leader and followers – a covenant of sorts from which the movement as a whole gains strength. This cult-figure directorship adds to the challenge facing the government forces combating Sendero. Although internal squabbling may cause the Peruvian army to falter, the insurgency has a continually unified front spearheaded by Guzmán. In sum, the Sendero leader is looked upon as larger-than-life by his followers throughout Peru.

Guzmán's personal importance is undisputed, but Sendero Luminoso is structured in such a way that it probably would not perish if its leader were killed or incapacitated. Sendero has molded a cadre of well-trained individuals able and qualified to lead – in high-level positions – on a moment's notice. If Guzmán were captured, the movement might stumble momentarily while his lieutenants drew themselves together, but it appears unlikely that it would disintegrate entirely. Guzmán may be an important figurehead for the movement, but the party itself rests on a stable foundation of commitment extending from the national Sendero leadership – those who work directly with Guzmán – to the newest recruit. Despite the organization and commitment of the leadership and cadres of Sendero

Luminoso, the insurgency's actions and violent tactics are alienating the very same sectors of the populace it claims to represent.

Vision of Utopia: A New Democratic Republic

Guzmán's new Peru would be a collectivist system, under the joint dictatorship of workers, peasants, and the petite bourgeoisie, all directed by the PCP-SL. Guzmán and his followers refer to the proposed system as the New Democratic Republic (*Republica Popular de la Nueva Democracia*). In essence, the republic is a Communist state based on the revolutionary theories of Mao and the indigenous institutions Mariátegui had so highly praised.

The concept of the New Democratic Republic is based to a great extent on a similar state structure conceived by Mao in 1940 called "New Democracy."[29] Mao realized, as did Lenin in Russia, that it would be difficult to transform China's long-standing social, political, and economic order into true communism. The New Democracy would therefore serve as a transitional system for the interim period, during which the colonialism and feudalism that had long fragmented and weakened China could be wiped away. The new system would unite the Chinese people under a joint dictatorship of all the anti-imperialist and anti-feudal classes. The term *New* Democracy served to distinguish Mao's idea of democratic government from the Western world's — what he refers to as *old* democracy. The Western system, Mao wrote, is only a facade used by the bourgeoisie to oppress the common people. The actual differences in class status are cleverly concealed under the mantle of "citizenship," allowing the elite to exploit the masses at will. Mao's New Democracy, in contrast, combined three elements: New Democratic politics, New Democratic economics, and New Democratic culture. The New Democracy would introduce authentic equality among the populace and clear the way for the ultimate advent of true communism.

The first step in implementing the New Democracy was to replace the deeply ingrained politics of Japanese imperialism and ancient "warlord" feudalism with Mao's New Democratic politics. A joint dictatorship was formed to rule the country that combined members of all the revolutionary classes—the proletariat, the peasantry, the intelligentsia, and the petite bourgeoisie. The leaders and organs of the central government were to be elected by a five-tiered series of congresses, ranging from the national people's congress to the township people's congress. In such a system, all were to have an equal voice in government, regardless of ethnic origin, education, property ownership, or gender.

Along the same lines, the implementation of a New Democratic economy also required significant changes for greater economic equality among the populace. In the new Chinese economy, the largest commercial enterprises—banks, factories, and sizable industries—were nationalized to deprive private capital of its political influence. Large feudal landholdings were expropriated and distributed among peasants who held little or no land. During this phase of development, however, private land ownership was still permitted, even among the wealthy peasants, as long as the quantity of land was not excessive. In fact, most rural land remained in private hands, although some state cooperatives were established. Here again, Mao essentially followed Lenin's guide by restricting capital holdings and equalizing land ownership so that no one class could control others. Realizing that China was not yet ready for absolute state ownership, however, he left small and medium parcels of land and certain commercial enterprises in private hands. As Chairman Mao's aspirations for China radicalized, however, private holdings were eventually seized by the state and placed under the mandate of newly formed peasant cooperatives; the nation was thereby brought closer to his vision of an ideal Communist order.[30]

Finally, the New Democratic culture reflected the new politics and the new economy. Mao insisted that the existing culture, one he termed feudal and imperialistic, be displaced by adherence to a Marxist series of beliefs based on scientific fact. These new beliefs would morally back the new state, inculcating in the population a spiritual bond to the concept of economic and social equality. Under the New Democratic system, the truth would no longer be gleaned from the "feudal and superstitious ideas" that had oppressed the Chinese for centuries, but rather from objective theories and practice. Religion—Marx's "opiate of the masses"—would no longer play a role in the lives of the people.

Although all three elements of the New Democracy are based in socialism, the New Democratic system itself was not yet entirely socialist or Communist. The primary goal, it should be remembered, was only to clear the path for true communism.

Guzmán approached the Peruvian situation differently. Although he clearly based his New Democratic Republic on Mao's New Democracy, he differs radically by not planning for a moderate interim stage between the fall of the existing state and the advent of communism. On the contrary, Guzmán's plans for Peru are far more radical. From the few available documents attributed to him, the New Democratic Republic appears to be an end in itself. Guzmán essentially refuses to recognize the importance of allowing a quasi-capitalist period of growth in which to develop the country—a step that Mao considered essential. Instead, paralleling Mao's great leap forward, he has planned for Peru to plunge almost directly into a Communist society. "Our goal," writes Guzmán, "is Communism—the only unsubstitutable society, without exploiters nor exploited, without oppressors nor oppressed, without classes, without state, without arms, without wars. . . ."[31]

The primary difference between the two systems is economic. Although Mao's New Democracy entails nationalization of the largest capitalist enterprises, Guzmán anticipates nationalization of all means of production. By allowing no private holdings, he believes the root cause of class differences will be eliminated. Any remaining vestiges of social or economic rank will be abrogated through popular education; those unable to adapt to the new system will be executed.[32] For Guzmán, the New Democratic Republic in Peru has already begun to emerge. Guzmán sees the popular committees (*comités populares*), which administer towns within areas under Sendero control, and support bases (*bases de apoyo*) as bastions of the "New Power" that will one day triumph in Peru.[33]

In planning for the transition to the New Democratic Republic, Guzmán accrued tremendous benefits from a series of developments that enabled him to bypass obstacles that had confronted Mao. The Peru of Mariátegui's day, like China, was a semifeudal, semicolonial country. During the late 1960s and early 1970s, however, the loosely conceived and poorly managed reforms of the Velasco regime in effect began the revolutionary process for Guzmán. The Sendero leader did not have to dismantle feudalism and undertake nationalization of foreign holdings; those two goals had largely been achieved already.

The political and economic reforms implemented during the military regimes of General Juan Velasco Alvarado (1968–1975) and General Francisco Morales Bermúdez (1975–1980) are among the most profound in modern Peruvian history. Velasco began the reform process immediately after ousting President Fernando Belaúnde Terry in 1968 with a sweeping agrarian reform law aimed at transforming the agrarian structure in the country and destroying the *latifundia*.[34] This policy, characterized by the slogan, "land to those who work it," allowed the government to expropriate the hacienda land and distribute possession of it to the rural poor.[35] The redistribution process was administered by government agencies and resulted in the formation of numerous cooperatives and the Societies of Social Agrarian Interests (Sociedades Agrarias de Interés Social, or SAIS). To help workers in the industrial sector, Velasco passed the Industrial Community (*Comunidad Industrial*) law that pretended to integrate workers more fully into the economic system by allowing them to share in both the management responsibilities and profits of the corporations that employed them. Finally, in an effort to cut Peru's ties to foreign capital, Velasco nationalized foreign industries in the country. Especially hard hit were oil and mining interests. Extensive holdings of the International Petroleum Corporation, Occidental, and Royal Dutch Shell were expropriated and merged to form PetroPeru. The government also took a controlling interest in the Cerro de Pasco Mining Corporation and the Marcona Copper Corporation—two of Peru's major metals exporters. Morales Bermudez continued the reform process by liberalizing political laws. To prepare the state for the upcoming 1980 elections, he introduced legislation that lowered the voting age to 18 and extended the right to vote to the illiterate.

Good intentions aside, these reforms ultimately caused many new problems. The agricultural cooperatives proved unable to support themselves; even the most prosperous relied heavily upon government subsidies. The new industrial laws made the hiring and firing of personnel an ordeal in the private sector and negatively affected production and property ownership. Peru's international borrowing expanded as the nation underwent rapid industrialization.[36] But perhaps the most important legacy from the military governments lay in the agricultural and industrial sectors. There the government's widespread promises to introduce a new system that would more fairly incorporate all citizens began to ring hollow as the reforms failed to develop as planned. The unmet promises, however, remained in the minds of many.

Thus Peru legally underwent some of the reforms that Mariátegui had suggested decades earlier. Although the reforms were largely unsuccessful, they nevertheless were aimed at substantially lessening the feudalistic and colonial nature of the nation's socioeconomic system. Guzmán turned this situation to Sendero's advantage and fashioned a strategy by which Peru, guided by Sendero Luminoso, would shed the stumbling state system and take the great leap forward into the New Democratic Republic.

3

Strategy: Achieving the
New Democratic Republic

The Popular War

Sendero Luminoso plans to bring Peru into the New Democratic Republic through a political and military struggle known as the "popular war." Its primary offensive weapon is the popular guerrilla army, whose members are drawn from the rural and urban underclasses. Strategy and direction are provided by the Sendero hierarchy; the central committee drafts general objectives and allows regional committees to define them more specifically. The popular war, as conceived by Guzmán, is composed of five phases, each bringing the party and the nation one step closer to the new state:

1. *Agitation and propaganda.* The purpose of this stage is to raise class consciousness and agitate the population, exacerbating existing class conflicts and calling attention to income inequalities and the "corrupt" system.

2. *Sabotage and guerrilla action.* This stage involves increased military action, directed for the most part against property belonging to the state and large companies. Sendero hopes this action will further weaken an already trembling economy, leading more people to become frustrated with the difficult living conditions and turn to the insurgency as an answer.

3. *Generalized violence and guerrilla warfare*. In this stage, support for the Sendero Luminoso movement spreads throughout the country. Increased violence further shakes the existing economic structure and widespread violence erupts. Senderistas and Sendero leaflets claim that this stage was reached in 1982, though the government's establishment of emergency military zones the following year in Ayacucho and Apurímac has somewhat slowed Sendero's violent advance in the primary region. Sendero has spread to other regions, however.

4. *Conquest and expansion of support bases*. As more and more people and territory fall under Sendero control, they are converted into "support bases," from which additional Sendero conquests are initiated. In these zones, such as Ayacucho, Apurímac, and Huancavelica, the local populations have been heavily indoctrinated with radical ideology. Although government counterinsurgency efforts in these regions may have subtracted from the total area under Sendero control, severe military repression and excesses have also had the adverse effect of turning more people to the rebellion. Sendero Luminoso claims to have secured support bases in the Andean highlands, the Huallaga Valley, and principal coastal cities.

5. *The fall of the cities and total collapse of the state*. Following basic Maoist strategy, Sendero Luminoso plans to strangle successive cities into submission as the rural populace unifies in its support of the insurgency. Supply routes into cities would be cut off and guarded until the urban areas have little choice but to surrender to Sendero control. As the major cities fall, the state would theoretically collapse. This strategy has undergone major modifications recently as Sendero has adopted more urban-oriented tactics.[1]

These stages are not detached or mutually exclusive; all function simultaneously. Theoretically, any of the various steps may proceed at the same time; agitation, propaganda, sabotage, and guerrilla warfare may continue in some areas even as bases of support are secured and cities encircled in others. Sendero reasons that a continuous assault on all fronts – psychological, economic, social, and military – will lead the state to capitulate, if only through exhaustion. By 1988, Peruvian political analysts thought that the movement had entered the fourth stage, because support bases have been established in at least 15 of Peru's 24 departments.[2]

Revolutionary violence – terrorism, sabotage, and guerrilla warfare – plays a prominent role in Sendero's strategy for toppling the state. This emphasis results from both the movement's adherence to Marxist-Leninist ideology and President Gonzalo's own particular interpretation of Peruvian history. First, following the movement's interpretations of Communist theory discussed above, Sendero accepts the notion that the transition to a "higher" system (communism) requires a revolutionary struggle. The scant Sendero literature available states openly that the "oppressed" will not be able completely to overcome the "oppressors" without armed conflict.[3] Accordingly, all theories of bringing about a socialist state through parliamentary reform are disavowed. It is therefore not surprising that, when President Alan García made earnest attempts to establish contact and hold dialogue with the insurgency in 1985, he was hostilely rebutted. Even Peru's registered leftist parties are considered illegitimate by Sendero leaders, who commonly refer to them as "parliamentary cretins," in spite of the fact that their goals are mutual.[4]

The Sendero Luminoso leadership also appeals to Peruvian history to support its inclination toward violence. According to Abimael Guzmán, the Peruvian people have always taken up arms to support or fight for their rights. He cites, among other examples, the battles against the invading Incas (the inherent contradiction is overlooked), the uprisings against the Spanish conquistadores, and, finally, the war against the Spanish for independence. Now, explains Guzmán, the Peruvian people must once again assert their freedom in a violent and vindictive war against the Peruvian government and those controlling the country's economy, whom he terms the "puppets of imperialism."

Destabilizing the Existing Order

The first step of the popular war is to destabilize the standing socioeconomic order through a variety of strategies, both psychological and military. If this societal superstructure and the entrenched dominant classes controlling it are to be overthrown, they must first be weakened or debilitated. To accomplish this goal, Sendero has devised a program that will raise the class consciousness of the peasants and workers, exacerbating the long-standing dissension, distrust, and social resentment these people feel. The program, begun at the grass-roots level in Ayacucho and neighboring departments in the 1970s, has now been elevated to a national campaign conducted through informal indoctrination classes known as popular schools (*escuelas populares*). At the same time that these popular schools are "educating" the public, acts of guerrilla sabotage and terrorism further weaken Peru's already precarious national stability. As the state becomes successively weaker and, simultaneously, the lower and middle classes become increasingly indoctrinated and polarized, a flood of revolutionary sentiment is expected to wash over the country, sweeping Sendero Luminoso into power.

Propaganda

Sendero's success to date is largely a result of its ability to spread ideology and beliefs throughout the population. Nine years ago, few outside of Ayacucho had ever heard of Sendero Luminoso; today, small children in Lima's shanty towns recite Sendero slogans as if they were nursery rhymes.[5] The emphasis of the information Sendero disseminates so exhaustively is two-pronged: Sendero stresses the inadequacy of the present state, raising class consciousness and aggravating existing feelings of injustice. With this powerful background in place, Sendero then outlines in glowing terms its plans for the future—a prosperous people's state in which all will flourish.

As one might imagine, there is no lack of grievances against the Peruvian government. The country's faltering economy lends itself particularly well to exploitation by Sendero Luminoso. With inflation skyrocketing from 70 percent in 1982 to 1,722 percent in 1988 and 2,775 percent in 1989, all Peruvians have been affected by the deep slump in buying power; the lower and middle classes, however, have been hit the hardest.[6] The precipitous decline in real wages has led to widespread anxiety and irritation, an environment of general distrust that Sendero has easily manipulated to its advantage. In contrast to the steadily worsening state of affairs in present-day Peru, Sendero propaganda speaks in sweeping terms of a new state in which all will have opportunity and wealth, all will take part in governing the state, and ethnic and class separations will be erased. The feasibility of such a state, an altogether separate matter, is not always considered.

The ideology that Sendero spreads, however, does not make the organization unique. Most insurgent movements base their propaganda on vilification of the present state and idealization of their personal visions of the future. What does make Sendero distinctive and dangerous is the unusual efficiency of the system it has devised to spread its doctrine and the ominous possibility that its ideology will become unshakably rooted with time because of this system.

Sendero's methods of indoctrination have developed alongside the movement itself. As discussed earlier, Guzmán and his followers began to diffuse their beliefs in the 1960s and 1970s while at UNSCH. First in private conversations, then in special study groups and seminars, the university became, in effect, Sendero's base camp. Conditioned students returned to their native rural communities and spread Guzmán's theories in easily understood terms among the peasants. Others, encouraged by Guzmán and his group, moved to neighboring departments, married into the communities, and, once trusted, began spreading Sendero ideology. This process of grass-roots indoctrination thus allowed the insurgency to gain extensive control in the provinces of Cangallo, Víctor Fajardo, La Mar, and Huanta in Ayacucho, and in the province of Andahuaylas in Apurímac. These provinces provided the precise socioeconomic conditions for Sendero's growth and development. They possessed schools (primarily at the initiative of the Indian community), but lacked a tradition of modern democratic organization. In addition, they had long been at odds with the Peruvian state. Sendero's approach in 1980–1982 clearly triumphed in Ayacucho.[7]

The next stage involved spreading the movement throughout Peru's university system, a project greatly aided by the FER. Using the existing mechanisms of the FER infrastructure, well-trained cadres of Sendero militants traveled throughout Peru encouraging the study of Mariátegui and the theory of armed struggle. Students were prompted to pursue the revolutionary path after graduation by returning to their native communities and spreading Sendero ideology, or by abetting the movement from within their respective professions by providing services – legal, medical, financial, psychological – that the insurgency might otherwise be unable to obtain.

To continue recruiting followers among the rural and urban substrata, Guzmán designed a system of informal indoctrination classes referred to as popular schools. These schools are taught by Sendero activists and militants – people well versed in the intellectual foundations of the movement. The schools' curriculum concentrates on Mariátegui's interpretations of Peruvian reality, the unjust and corrupt nature of the existing socioeconomic system, and the future as Sendero plans it. The teaching style is tailored to the receiving audience: illiterate peasants, for example, receive simple and easily understood lectures far different from those given to university students.

Another large and important sector of the population particularly susceptible to the contagious enthusiasm of the Sendero indoctrinators are the thousands of secondary school students unable to pass the demanding entrance exams required for matriculation into Peruvian universities. A total number of 247,670 students were denied entrance in 1987. (Of 217,679 students applying to public universities in 1987, 36,489 or 16.7 percent were accepted; of 95,131 students applying to private universities, 28,651 or 30.2 percent were accepted.[8] These students, mostly teenagers, have no alternative but to try and find work—a daunting task given Peru's collapsed economy. Denied entrance to a university, most perceive no further opportunities for economic or social advancement. Sendero Luminoso offers an outlet for the immense frustration and hostility these young men and women feel toward the system, energy that can be prodded effectively into ruthless violence. (The numbers and locations of the popular schools are under investigation by the police.)

Psychologically, the popular schools provide these sectors of Peruvian populace with a sense of hope—something that no other institution, governmental or private, has been able to do.[9] The schools, as well as the camaradie they inspire, have cast a thin shaft of light into an otherwise dark existence and have stimulated a type of psychological dependency. When a young man or woman can enter an extremely poor rural or urban community and speak confidently about a bright future, a future of opportunity that will end exploitation and corruption of the system, that person inspires hope where it might otherwise never surface. Those listening (displaced migrants, unwed mothers, and the underemployed and unemployed of all ages) grasp the fact that they are being presented with a chance to become part of something—to "belong," to be needed, and to give their lives an otherwise unobtainable significance.[10] The warmth and sense of personal importance imparted by the popular schools contrasts starkly to the indifferent outside world and encourages dependency on Sendero. Longheld hostility and frustration toward society may now be channeled toward bettering it by aiding Sendero Luminoso in forging a new Peru.

Support Bases

By appearing to display a real understanding of the situation in which Peru's massive underclass finds itself and by promising confidently that this condition can indeed be altered, Sendero has been able to recruit support bases (*bases de apoyo*) throughout the country. The term "support base" refers essentially to a geographic region in which portions of the population have committed themselves to backing the insurgency. Assistance takes the form of foodstuffs, safe shelter, clothing, transportation, and, on occasion, arms, medicine, and money. Perhaps most significant, though, is the degree to which some communities have committed manpower. Not only do the current youth join Sendero's ranks enthusiastically, but both the very young and the very old are enlisted for the revolution. When asked by a reporter what they wished to do with their lives, highland children in Ayacucho responded, "Yo quiero ser terruco"—"I want to be a terrorist." At the opposite end of the spectrum, many elderly men and women are equally committed to supporting Sendero's revolutionary efforts—if not motivated by ideological commitment, perhaps by fear or knowledge of their children's involvement.[11]

Secure support bases can now be found along the entire north-south stretch of Peru. Beginning in the Andean highlands, Sendero has established bases in Ayacucho, Apurímac, and Huancavelica. From these initial bases, the insurrection has spread in every direction. Other highland bases were founded in the southern departments of Cusco and portions of Puno. Then, pushing north, the movement started coastal bases in the departments of Lima and Lambayeque, all the while continuing to add highland support in the departments of Junín, La Libertad, Pasco, Ancash, and Cajamarca. Extremely effective rain-forest support bases were then founded in San Martín and Huánuco. These latter conquests are especially important, for they illustrate with startling clarity how Sendero adapts itself to the peculiarities of a region's existing socioeconomic situation to recruit the local population more effectively. At present, Sendero claims to control the Andean corridor — that is, the entire length of the Andes mountain range reaching from the north to the south of Peru.[12]

Tactics

Once established, support bases serve as launch sites for the next phase of Sendero strategy — guerrilla warfare. This stage of the insurrection is composed of three parts: sabotage, terrorism, and open guerrilla warfare. Through the collective application of the three offensive mediums, the movement has weakened the incumbent "reactionary" regime further and goaded the military into additional repression of the urban and rural underclasses. Although Sendero has not initiated an open, outright war with the government, its guerrilla warfare campaign has disrupted the economy and caused the government to appear ineffectual, unrepresentative, and oppressive. Neither President Belaúnde nor President Alan García Pérez has been able to mount a genuinely successful defense or deterrent, despite heavy rhetoric to the contrary.

Sabotage. Sabotage involves the destruction of property, either public or private, and the decline in productivity that may result. Sendero's use of this medium to advance its cause is now legendary. It has cost the state and private enterprise millions of dollars in damages, draining funds that might have been used for desperately needed social and development programs.[13] Furthermore, because many of the movement's destructive ventures must have been inside jobs requiring high levels of technical expertise or security access, an atmosphere of suspicion and distrust has been created in both the public and private sectors. In 1984, for example, Sendero toppled eight high-tension electricity towers in the Mantaro Valley, plunging a full one third of the nation into a complete power blackout. This act, and many others like it, could not have been accomplished without inside help — in this case from numerous employees of the state electric company.

The insurrection concentrates on sabotage of this type for both economic and psychological reasons. Forcing the government to repair or replace the pipeline, bridges, roads, electrical equipment, and other infrastructure exhausts funds set aside for relief, social programs, and regional investment. Simultaneously, Sendero draws attention to the apparent inefficiency of the government, which can neither control the insurrection nor protect its own assets. The resulting climate of chaos and discontent has a deep psychological impact on the nation. Many marginal groups, having lost all faith in the government, see no alternative but to turn to Sendero.

The extent of the damage for which Sendero is responsible is considerable. Primary targets include the assets of large multinational companies and just about anything associated with the government of Peru.[14] The movement diligently chooses acts that not only will require expensive repairs or replacement, but also will affect large portions of the population, inducing frustration with the government's inability to maintain order. In 1984, for example, Sendero dynamited Oleoducto Norperunano's tremendously expensive oil pipeline that carries oil from the Amazon to the coast. Several lengths of the pipeline were completely destroyed, and the incident created multimillion-dollar losses in replacement costs and lost exports. Electric plants are also among Sendero's favored targets. Besides the Mantaro Valley incident, guerrillas have also incapacitated major electricity facilities at Cañón del Pato and Marcona. After one of these incidents, in which the entire city of Lima was blacked out on Abimael Guzmán's birthday (December 4), a giant bonfire in the shape of a hammer and sickle was lit on a hillside overlooking the city. In a similar action, to demonstrate its opposition to the Catholic Church, Sendero militants blacked-out the Lima airport just minutes before the Pope was to land for his widely publicized visit in January 1985. As airport engineers raced to restore emergency runway lighting, yet another immense hammer and sickle bonfire appeared on the hill over Lima.

In 1989 alone, Sendero downed 335 high-tension electric towers, which cost the nation U.S. $42 million in repairs. Between 1980 and 1989, Sendero downed 1,205 electric pylons. A January 1990 press release by Electro-Perú—the Peruvian National Electric Company—reported damages of U.S. $600 million during the 1980–1989 period. As of early 1990, Lima copes with limited electric power; various sectors of the city are served by turn, each receiving only a few hours of power a day. Thus, productivity at industrial centers, as well as in businesses and administrative services, is severely hampered by the lack of electricity.[15]

Terrorism. Acts of terrorism threaten or cause a loss of life among innocent noncombatants for the purpose of achieving political goals. As Charles Maechling explained in the *Foreign Service Journal*, "The legitimate guerrilla fighter sticks to military targets, but if civilians are singled out as victims, or targets are selected in such a way that makes loss of innocent life inevitable, he or she is considered a terrorist and a criminal outlaw."[16] From 1980 to 1988, some 7,700 Peruvian civilians have died in Sendero-related incidents, according to official statistics (see figure 2). The real toll on human life is much higher. By 1989, deaths were believed to be 15,000.[17] Terrorist attacks may either be launched indiscriminately against victims so unfortunate as simply to be present or may be launched purposefully against targets that, for the terrorist, somehow represent "the hated quality of the enemy" (anything representing the state and government). The latter type of terrorist act, termed "symbolic transference" by psychologists, is exemplified by Sendero's attacks on foreign researchers and tourists who, for the insurgents, represent the evils of capitalism and imperialism.[18]

FIGURE 2
Dead and Wounded in Terrorist Incidents, 1980–1988

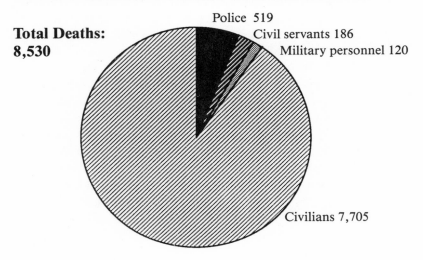

Total Deaths:
8,530

Police 519
Civil servants 186
Military personnel 120

Civilians 7,705

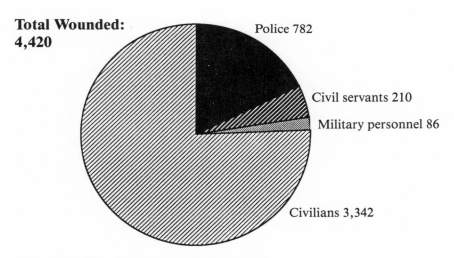

Total Wounded:
4,420

Police 782

Civil servants 210

Military personnel 86

Civilians 3,342

Source: Ministry of the Interior, July 28, 1988.

Sendero's heavy reliance on terrorism serves two purposes. First, the movement claims it is exercising justice by destroying the "enemies of the people." By targeting those to whom Guzmán refers as bourgeoisie "elites" (that is, wealthy merchants, landowners, high government officials, and others who cooperate with these people), the insurgency leadership insists it is "burning the palms of the enemy's blood stained hands."[19] Second, but equally important, terrorism, like sabotage, puts tremendous psychological and economic stress on the populace in areas of heavy Sendero activity. Living under the constant threat of violence demoralizes the population and even further undermines trust in the government. At first glance, Sendero's targets may appear to be random or chance: they come from all levels of society, all parts of the country, and even include some foreigners. When examined more closely, however, a definite pattern emerges, emphasizing again Sendero's acute attention to detail. Broadly speaking, the movement's targets may be separated into two categories: personal and collective. The former includes specific assassination attempts and personal "warnings"; the latter, bombings and attacks on towns or military installations.

High-ranking members of the armed forces are especially attractive targets for Sendero. Besides holding a position in the government, these individuals represent the established social order Sendero has declared the enemy. Rear Admiral Carlos Ponce Canessa is among the insurgency's more notable victims. A brilliant and highly visible navy official, Ponce was murdered in his car in May 1986. While the officer was stopped at a traffic light, four men stepped out from behind trees. Two fired into the car while the others tossed dynamite underneath it. Although wounded by the shots, Ponce was able to draw his own pistol and fire twice before the explosions detonated. Sendero's rationale for the assassination was most likely a result of Ponce's involvement with the Peruvian navy's elite operations team, the Infantes de Marina. This team was accused of committing serious human-rights violations while maintaining territory recovered from Sendero in Huanta. Although Ponce was not involved with the Infantes de Marina while they were in Huanta, he was later put in charge of restoring their public image – an assignment that gave him extensive media exposure. Sendero publicized the assassination as retribution; they were "avenging" the wrongdoings that had occurred in Huanta. As an important government official, Ponce provided the high visibility factor the insurgency sought, although he was personally involved only through association.[20]

Attacks on people who are associated with a particular economic, social, or political group are a common Sendero tactic. As in the case of Rear Admiral Ponce, the movement sees these measures as punishment or retribution for past "crimes against the people," such as working with the government, the multinational corporations, or the political parties to which the insurgency is opposed. An assassination attempt was made in October 1986 against Vice Admiral Gerónimo Cafferata Marazzi simply because he held a high state position. As Cafferata approached a street corner and began to slow his car down, two men and a woman stepped out from behind a newsstand and began firing automatic weapons at him. Although not immediately killed, Cafferata sustained severe injuries that required his transfer to the United States for medical care. He died while undergoing treatment. All three terrorists were apprehended. They later explained that there was no motive for their action apart from that of assassinating a high-level military official.[21]

In another case – a collective attack – eight Soviet sailors suffered severe injuries when a bomb exploded beneath their table in a bazaar near the port of El Callao. One of the sailors lost both legs and an arm. Once again, the target (the sailors) appealed to the insurgency only because of its association with an entity the movement opposes – the Soviet Union. Sendero Luminoso's ideological feud with the "revisionist" Soviets has been widely publicized in Sendero literature and the popular schools. By attacking the Soviet sailors, Sendero was declaring the nationalistic emphasis of its movement to the press, the government, the people, and any foreign countries that might be watching.

Symbolic attacks such as these occur often throughout Peru. The Chinese, Soviet, and U.S. embassies have all been attacked numerous times. Sendero achieved a new degree of notoriety when, in June 1986, a bomb exploded on the train that carries tourists — mainly Americans and Europeans — from Cusco to the Inca ruins at Machu Picchu. Some 40 people were injured and eight were killed, including one American. This attack was viewed as a desperate show of strength after the massive prison uprisings of June 18–19, 1986, in which 266 Senderistas were killed. In these cases and many similar ones, Sendero's intention was to strike back at representatives of the "imperialist" countries it holds partially responsible for the conditions in Peru or of the "revisionist" nations it claims have "betrayed the revolution." Additionally, attacks in which foreigners are injured or killed attract both national and international media attention, contributing to the loss of faith in the incumbent government and enhancing perceptions of Sendero's power and reach.[22]

Retribution is also levied against members of the Peruvian subclasses that ally themselves with those Sendero considers enemies. Elected officials who refuse to resign or turn over power to Sendero upon request are routinely executed, often in front of the towns that elected them. The insurgency has been known to attack entire communities, committing brutal murders and destroying property, because the townspeople obeyed Peruvian law by participating in government anti-Sendero programs. Others have been raided simply for expressing reticence about supporting the insurgency, if only for economic reasons. In September 1986, for example, Sendero militants attacked Cochas, a small, impoverished Ayacucho village. The men and women of Cochas feebly tried to defend themselves with rocks, knives, and farming implements, but were rapidly overcome by the guerrillas' automatic firearms. Eight people were killed and the entire village's some 65 structures were burned down. The people of Cochas were victimized because they had followed the government's order to form a peasant defense patrol.[23]

The case of Cochas is not an isolated incident; there are many others like it. The Sendero leadership has determined that if communities do not join the insurgency by will, they therefore qualify as "counterrevolutionaries" and should be punished to serve as an example to others. Unfortunately, the government is unable to defend all the communities that have remained loyal, leading many to feel as if they have been abandoned by the state. As a result, many of these towns are broken apart by fear and internal conflicts. Others, such as Cochas, have been destroyed by Sendero. Of the 32 communities located in the same military zone as Cochas (Guarnición Militar de Chacco), 17 communities composed of about 5,000 families have ceased to exist in their traditional state since the violence began in 1980. Some have packed their meager belongings and moved north to the jungle, a climate and agricultural region for which they are invariably unprepared. Others have transferred to urban centers such as Lima, where they encounter a brutal social situation and extreme difficulty in finding employment. The remaining communities persevere where they are, vacillating between commitment to the military or Sendero, realizing that neither choice is likely to provide protection, while both invite attack. During a five-week period in 1988, the villages of Chacas, Rumi-Rumi, and Huayanay, located in the province of La Mar, as well as the Ayacucho villages of Chacani and Pocomarca in the province of Vilcashuamán, had suffered bloody attacks by Sendero that resulted in the deaths of 72 people.[24]

Open guerrilla warfare. Finally, Sendero Luminoso uses open guerrilla warfare to advance its revolution militarily. This type of aggression allows the insurgency to terrorize some sectors of the population into complicity, punish others that support the government, and protect areas already sustaining the movement. Open guerrilla warfare further provides Sendero with an effective method of irritating the government through dispersed attacks that dilute military concentrations and provoke added official repression.

Guzmán and his lieutenants have adhered closely to the writings of Mao in developing their alarmingly effective guerrilla strategy. Although Sendero Luminoso is vastly inferior to the state in military armaments and trained battalions of troops, this liability has been overcome through heavy concentration on strategic planning. Surprise attacks upon limited or weakened government forces ensures strategic advantage in each campaign. Guzmán has realized, however, that strategic success is only half the battle; Sendero must also win the hearts of the people.

To turn the tide of popular opinion in its favor, the movement has invested heavily in the popular schools and other indoctrination enterprises. In the Sendero rationale, once the masses have been recruited, the government and its forces will have lost their primary base of support. Taking this idea one step further is the corollary that the masses and the revolutionary army should become indistinguishable. In Mao's metaphor, "the popular masses are like water, and the army is like a fish. How can it be said that when there is water, a fish will have difficulty in preserving its existence?"[25] Once a large degree of popular favor has been won, the distinction between the revolutionaries and the masses becomes muddled. As a result, guerrilla forays and recruitment missions become streamlined as the revolutionary fighters and the masses become increasingly indistinguishable.

Indoctrination forums also provide a steady stream of malleable recruits. Once saturated with Guzmán's doctrine, Sendero militants exhibit extraordinarily high morale, perceiving the war as a personal and vindictive response to the oppression of their ethnic group or social class. Those participating in Sendero's struggle are aware that the combat will be prolonged; Guzmán has stated repeatedly that the war might last 50, even 100, years. Sendero's heavy ideological base therefore plays an important role in anchoring the movement and ensuring its longevity. People joining the insurgency are convinced that they are fighting for what is right, for justice. Such ideological passion leads militants to disregard their own safety completely when in pursuit of a Sendero objective; they literally consider their own lives expendable. Senderistas believe that if the war is lost, the Peruvian situation will indeed become worse. Guzmán's ideology has portrayed Sendero Luminoso as the only salvation for Peru.

"Armed struggle," wrote Guzmán, "is the only revolutionary road possible and it is already open."[26] Sendero has turned to armed conflict because its leadership utterly rejects the notion that parliamentary reform can prove sufficiently radical to bring about constructive change in Peru. "El poder nace del fusil" is the Spanish version of Mao's statement that "political power grows out of the barrel of a gun."[27] It has been adopted by Sendero as a slogan to initiate the armed struggle against the state.

According to Sendero Luminoso, the guerrilla war develops in three fundamental stages: (1) the initiation of the guerrilla war, (2) the securing and expanding of support bases, and (3) the development of further support bases. These steps are not chronologically separate, as they blend together and mesh with political progress in advancing the movement's objectives. The guerrilla war itself falls within phases two, three, and four of the popular war discussed earlier.

The first phase—the initiation of the guerrilla war—especially depends upon political success in a target area. The main objective of this step is to buttress popular education initiatives with military action. Once the Sendero leadership has chosen a region it wishes to secure, the popular education movement begins there with the aim of arousing the inhabitants to action. After a certain amount of indoctrination, the "students" begin to show signs of agitation, and the introductory military phase is initiated. Local police, military, and government officials are threatened or assassinated, police stations are besieged, and supplies are looted. Landowners and those involved in large-scale land administration (cooperatives) are also targeted, as are the land and developments they operate. Aside from destabilizing the incumbent powers in the region, these first guerrilla actions reinforce the teachings of the popular schools, translating classroom rhetoric into reality. If the Sendero plan is successful, the combined tactics will lead to a power vacuum, clearing the way for the second stage of the guerrilla war—the securing and expansion of support bases. Successful or not, however, it will lead almost certainly to regional military repression by the Peruvian army. Either way, Sendero Luminoso comes out ahead.

Sendero has designated the second stage of its guerrilla war the "securing and expansion of support bases." Regions in which early Sendero initiatives were well received are now pushed toward becoming full support bases. Here again, the political and military strategies are heavily enmeshed, each complementing the other in efforts to bolster Sendero allegiance among the populace of a target region. According to Sendero doctrine, once the movement has garnered a significant degree of support, "a great qualitative leap" (*gran salto*) will occur. At this time there will emerge a "New Democratic Republic" in the area—a new state that will struggle with the existing structure for complete geopolitical control of the region. Sendero literature describes the "new state" as a complete "second republic" that will attempt to dismantle the establishment on all levels—economic, political, and, especially, military. One of the primary duties of the new state is that of disseminating the guerrilla war—spreading it among the populace as Sendero seeks to gain complete control of the region and expand to others.[28]

Once the great leap has occurred, the popular guerrilla army begins to initiate direct attacks against government forces in addition to the ongoing terrorism and sabotage. By its adherence to Mao's principles, Sendero has a definite advantage at this stage. Paralleling the initiatives of the Vietcong during the Vietnam conflict, the insurgency has capitalized upon the knowledge of new recruits and militants about the locales in which they are operating and their personal relationships with the inhabitants of these regions. A January 1988 *El Diario* newspaper insert prepared by Sendero Luminoso and sold freely in newsstands points out that the design of the government's antiterrorist initiatives are drawn from the Vietnam War, certain Central American conflicts, and the Peruvian antiguerrilla movement of the mid-1960s. According to Sendero, "This is counterrevolutionary strategy that has been defeated repeatedly—smashed and completely destroyed by the popular war—demonstrating to the world once and again the superiority of the proletarian strategy against imperialism."[29]

Sendero's military plans are so engineered that they are strategically centralized but tactically decentralized, a principle that allows Guzmán and his cupola (Sendero's national directorship) to conduct the war while local commanders plan battles.[30] Aside from the commanders, a great number of the militants are drawn from the local population. Because these people do not wear uniforms and because they are familiar with the geographic area where they are working, they are able to melt into the local population or the terrain with consummate ease once expeditions have been completed. The rebels rely heavily on the use of surprise attacks on weak or unprepared army detachments, a tactic that enables them to inflict serious and exhausting damages to the Peruvian military.[31] After such attacks, the guerrillas disappear into surrounding hills or towns, leaving the army no opportunity for countermeasures.[32] The military is further hampered because Sendero offers it no real targets: the guerrillas usually work out of towns and villages and have no base camps that can be attacked. Sendero augments the potency of its surprise attacks by advancing simultaneously on multiple fronts.[33] Time-coordinated but independent offensives are made in different geographial areas, utilizing maneuvers that tire and disperse government forces. On the occasions that the police and the army have been able to defeat a Sendero detachment or recapture an area, victory was inevitably overshadowed by the insurgency's remarkable resiliency. Just as one region is brought under state control, another one or more will fall to Sendero. In the first year of insurgent activity alone, between April 1980 and May 1981, there were 482 incidents of Sendero militarism throughout the nation.[34] It is logistically daunting and physically exhausting for the police and military concurrently to defend the population and themselves against attack, maintain routine patrolling, and prevent impending offensives. Thus, through a variety of tactics, Sendero has produced tremendous frustration within the regular military, frustration that often leads to repression of the local population. As Mao and Guzmán understood, government action of this type alienates the people and actually works as a recruiting device for the movement.

The third stage of the guerrilla war—development of support bases—has apparently not yet been reached in any part of Peru. Its basic outline therefore remains rather vague. It is believed that this phase will involve consolidating the existing bases and using them to spread further Sendero Luminoso support and control throughout the remainder of the nation. Currently the insurrection has sympathizers in all but 4 of the country's 24 departments. The rebels claim to have developed a braid of influence reaching from Cajamarca, on the Ecuadorian border, to Puno, on the Bolivian border. If the insurgency's recruiting efforts continue to go well, an imbalance of popular allegiance could result that the present government will be unable to reverse. Once a majority of rural Peru has aligned itself with Sendero Luminoso, the stage will be set for what has been heralded as the final act of the popular war—encirclement of the cities and collapse of the state.

The Final Stage

The Fall of the Cities

Patterned after Mao's strategy, the final stage of the armed struggle originally called for a united rural population to rise up and encircle Peru's cities. As large cities fall in sequence, the existing state and government structure would topple in upon itself, wiping the slate clean so that Sendero would be free to construct its own new form of state. During 1988, however, this strategy was drastically restructured. Guzmán and other Sendero Luminoso leaders did not foresee the massive wave of urban migration that began in 1980 when Sendero surfaced and vastly accelerated over the next eight years. The people Sendero had planned to organize against the cities were now moving to the cities voluntarily.

Urban migration is neither new nor unique to Peru. Over the past 40 years, almost all Latin American nations have experienced this phenomenon to some degree. In most countries, people are leaving rural areas because it has become increasingly difficult to earn a living there. The mass media has also influenced urbanization, enticing rural inhabitants through television, movies, radio, and print with a "bright lights, big city" vision of urban life. The prospect of earning more money, enjoying a more glamorous lifestyle, and providing a better education for children has led many to move. Although all of these factors have undoubtedly influenced the urban migration of Peru's Andean population, the most powerful determinant of the demographic shift is that rural dwellers are fleeing the violence and unbearable living conditions created by the rise of Sendero Luminoso.

Pressures on the Rural Population

The escalating war has introduced a double-edged sword of terror to the countryside: on the one hand are Sendero's terrorist tactics; on the other, the heavy-handed repression of the Peruvian military. The rural populace is caught squarely in the middle. The nature of the situation, sadly, is one in which people are often forced to choose one side or the other, regardless of their desire to remain uninvolved. Once Sendero has penetrated an area and begun popular education, allegiance is exhorted from the local population, especially if some terrorist act (that is, the "execution" of a corrupt official, for example) has been committed on behalf of the community. Inhabitants are "asked" to attend classes and provide support, in the form of shelter, protection, and supplies, for the Senderistas. For people who struggle just to provide enough for their own families, such demands may constitute substantial hardship. Many peasants, however, prefer to do as the guerrillas ask rather than be labeled "government sympathizers," a characterization that may lead to execution.

The Peruvian government, on the other hand, has not legitimized itself in the eyes of the populace either. Like Sendero, it demands allegiance; if officials believe a community favors the insurrection, the army may impose indiscriminate repression. Even in cases where only one member of a community is found to be involved with Sendero Luminoso, the entire village population becomes suspect. Skittish army officers have been known to implement "protective" measures that protect little but extract a high price from the community in terms of patience and energy. To ease the difficulty of patrolling small but widely scattered peasant communities, the government has forced whole villages to move to other locations, leaving behind belongings and the land that they and their ancestors had tilled for centuries. In some cases two very distinct groups were forced to live together, causing immediate and obvious problems.

The war has affected rural life in other ways as well. Promised government assistance for agricultural, development, and social projects has never materialized as the state increasingly directs its efforts toward controlling Sendero. Teachers and medical staff, desperately needed throughout rural Peru, are now afraid to move to these areas. Both know that sooner or later they will be approached by Senderistas and asked to provide supplies or support of some kind. If they agree to help, they will be considered "committed" and thus in danger from the military. If they refuse, they will be marked by the insurgency as government sympathizers and treated accordingly—executed. In either case, citizens residing in rural areas are deprived of basic services and desperately needed government support.

When the burden of supporting Sendero militants, attending classes, and ignoring former friends or family members becomes too great; when it becomes impossible to earn a living and support one's children; when the squalor, overcrowding, disease, and malnutrition of the Civil Defense camps becomes unbearable; when the government abandons half-completed projects, and official promises to provide basic services come time and again to nothing; and when the stress of living in a militarized zone becomes overwhelming, people leave for the city. In a sense, this phenomenon might be more aptly termed rural flight than urban migration. The psychological pounding to which rural Peruvians are subjected in the crossfire of Sendero Luminoso and the government's flailing counterinsurgency measures has become too great for most to bear.

New Urban-Oriented Tactics

The Sendero Luminoso leadership has repeatedly shown itself to be adept at reading the social climate in which it is operating and adjusting its goals accordingly. Since late 1987, it has been aware of the change in the population of the countryside and how it affects the long-range strategy for encircling the cities. Obviously a massive rural insurrection that will topple the cities is now a less viable option than it may have been eight years ago. Sendero has further recognized that the cities, besides being the most politically conscious areas in the nation, are also populated by thousands of people living in miserable poverty – the category of people most easily provoked into revolutionary action.

The insurgency has therefore radically modified its strategy. Beginning in 1987, the movement experimented with new urban-oriented tactics. These overtures were well-accepted in the cities, encouraging the formulation of a more organized urban front. At the meeting of the Sendero Luminoso National Congress in February 1988, the congress decided to initiate a blanket increase in urban activity. A new final stage was introduced: "armed insurgency in the cities."[35] Sendero strategy is no longer to surround the cities and strangle them into submission; instead, the rebels plan to recruit so heavily within the urban areas that the government and the middle and upper classes will become totally isolated and ultimately collapse.

In a single step, then, Sendero Luminoso shifted from being primarily a rural movement to an urban one. Its plans no longer calls for a prolonged war in the countryside, but rather for a violent seduction of the populous urban underclass that will lead by the early 1990s to the collapse of Peru's major cities.[36] To this end Sendero has mounted a full-scale urban offensive. Operating primarily in Lima, militants have led meetings, classes, and lectures at the University of San Marcos. Public marches, a tactic never before used by Sendero, have been held all over the city. A heavily attended protest in March 1988 took place in the Plaza del Congreso, which is surrounded by the house of congress and located just blocks away from the Presidential Palace. The marchers were not swayed by the presence of large numbers of armed guards and tanks, who, in turn, did little more than hold back the crowds that turned out to watch.[37] Posters have been plastered throughout the city condemning the government and urging people to consider the Sendero alternative. Long documents explaining the Sendero Luminoso plan have been distributed at university campuses and in lower-class *barrios* (neighborhoods). And newspaper inserts have appeared regularly to explain Sendero and display the breadth of the Senderistas' diversity and dispersion. All of these actions have been accompanied by escalating sabotage and terrorism. Selective assassinations continue at an accelerated pace, as do power blackouts, which now occur almost daily.[38] The new urban assault has substantially complicated Peru's already precarious national situation. How the government deals with Sendero's urban initiative will be of paramount significance in the future.

4

Organization

One of Sendero's strengths lies in its high degree of organization; clearly, Sendero Luminoso is no loosely assembled group of revolutionaries. To the contrary, it is an intellectually based, hierarchical insurgency that may very well rival some large corporations in its sophisticated organization. Fundamentally, Sendero Luminoso operates on three distinct levels—national, regional, and local. Each of these divisions is buttressed by multiple layers of support sections, cells, and committees—some clandestine, some legal and legitimate.

Captured documents and individuals have revealed that Sendero held its most recent National Congress in February 1988. Government officials believe the meeting's agenda included discussion, evaluation, and criticism of the insurgency's basic strategy and progress to date. Besides Sendero's new emphasis on an urban front, the insurrection's top-level decision makers are believed to be pleased with the movement's latest accomplishments and strongly expect the revolution to triumph by the early 1990s.[1] Before this National Congress, Sendero is known to have held three similar reunions—in 1979, 1982, and 1985—where divergent positions regarding strategy and ideology were discussed and resolved.[2] General Assembly meetings such as these follow traditional Communist Party structure, providing a forum where criticisms can be aired, plans discussed, and policy set. The limited number of individuals attending these assemblies indicates that Sendero Luminoso makes high-level policy decisions in a hierarchical, not democratic, fashion. Moreover, these meetings demonstrate that the movement has the capacity to coordinate and inform on a national level.[3]

National and Regional Levels

Sendero Luminoso is directed nationally by the National Central Committee composed of Guzmán and his top lieutenants. This committee is responsible for making decisions on ideology, policy, and strategy affecting the entire Sendero Luminoso bloc of the PCP. Directly below the National Central Committee on the party's organizational flow chart are six regional committees—Eastern, Southern, Northern, Central, Metropolitan, and Primary—that, although independent, function according to national directives (see figure 3).

Each regional committee encompasses several departments and departmental subdivisions (provinces and districts). The one exception is the Metropolitan Regional Committee, comprising solely the provinces of Lima and Callao. Because the present population of Lima is thought to approach 7 million, the Metropolitan Regional Committee is of special importance and therefore does not extend to other departments. These regional committees are charged with the planning, evaluation, and execution of all Sendero activity—educational and military—occurring inside their boundaries. Within the party structure, regions are further broken down into zones, sectors, and cells, each with their own military detachments.

The Sendero leadership has wisely recognized that local people are better able, on the whole, to assess potential targets and the most effective times to attack than mem-

FIGURE 3
Organization of Sendero Luminoso

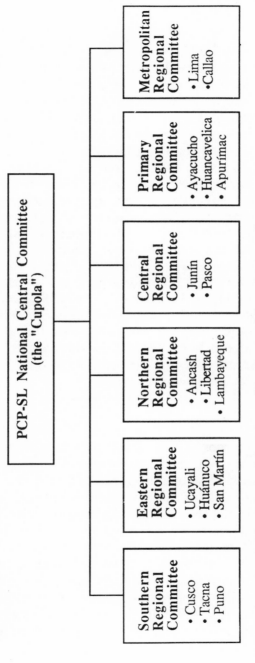

PCP-SL National Central Committee (the "Cupola")

Southern Regional Committee
• Cusco
• Tacna
• Puno

Eastern Regional Committee
• Ucayali
• Huánuco
• San Martín

Northern Regional Committee
• Ancash
• Libertad
• Lambayeque

Central Regional Committee
• Junín
• Pasco

Primary Regional Committee
• Ayacucho
• Huancavelica
• Apurímac

Metropolitan Regional Committee
• Lima
• Callao

Note: For a detailed breakdown of the Metropolitan Regional Committee, see figure 4.
Source: Data from Dirección Contra el Terrorismo (DIRCOTE), 1987, updated by the author.

bers of the national leadership, who may or may not have ever visited the area. Hence, the National Central Committee allows the regional commanders a considerable sphere of autonomy. This tactic alleviates much cumbersome bureaucracy and enables the regional committees to act with great efficiency; it has led to unusual military mobility and a high success ratio for Sendero operations. The Peruvian army, in contrast, is sluggish as a result of its top-heavy command structure and has found it difficult to undertake counteroffensives promptly. In spite of this high degree of regional freedom, however, the party is able to act in national unison when situations require or when the national leadership deems it necessary for the party to exhibit multiregional organization and power. Coordinated attacks are planned several times a year, commemorating Guzmán's birthday (December 4), Independence Day (July 28), and Heroes' Day (June 19, honoring the 256 Senderistas who died in the El Frontón and Lurigancho prison uprisings). This combination of personal initiative and party unity is one of Sendero's basic tenets. "In the party they teach us that we are not loose pearls," explained one captured militant, "but rather a pearl necklace."[4]

Metropolitan Level

Sendero Luminoso's Metropolitan Region is made up of Lima and Callao. In line with the insurgency's recent switch from a rural- to urban-oriented strategy, this region has become the focus of the movement's political and terrorist activities. Lima, the capital of Peru, and Callao, the nation's primary port, are both heavily populated and protected by the nation's police and military forces. As such, these locales present ideal opportunities for Sendero to exhibit its high level of organization and ability to strike quickly and effectively. Not coincidentally, these strengths also make the government's difficulty in countering or preventing insurgency initiatives blatantly apparent to inhabitants of the area.

Lima and Callao are actually distinguishable in name only; the two provinces compose one large metropolitan area. Sendero has divided the entire area into six subregions, designated by location (see figure 4) and directed by the Metropolitan Central Committee secretaries. These secretaries, all of whom were women from 1983 to 1985, also attend meetings of the Sendero Luminoso's National Central Committee, or "cupola."

Acting as emissary between the Metropolitan Central Committee and Lima's six zone leaders is the "coordinator." This individual maintains a post of great importance: besides serving as an intermediary between the Metropolitan Central Committee and the zone leaders, a function that protects the identities of both, he is also responsible for maintaining lists of the true names of all Sendero Luminoso members in Lima. (In Lima, as in all of Peru, Sendero militants and sympathizers know each other only by the *nom de guerre*, a device that effectively protects other members' identities and their families in case of capture.) Although the position of coordinator was once located below the Metropolitan Central Committee on the organization's flowchart, the coordinator may now actually sit on the committee itself.

Reporting directly to the Metropolitan Central Committee secretaries are four "special squads," which, by the nature of their duties, might also be termed "hit squads" or "death squads." The primary function of these squads, each of which is made up of three to four dedicated militants, is to carry out acts of sabotage or terrorism. Extensive studies of numerous attacks and assassinations compiled by the special police division charged with the investigation of terrorist activities, Dirección Contra el Terrorismo (DIRCOTE), have revealed that there is a basic pattern to most of the insurgency's urban assaults: each of the four special squads performs a specific, predetermined role.

Attacks or assassinations are initiated by the first special squad or "annihilation detachment." Members of this detail will typically pose on the street as innocent-looking

FIGURE 4
Organization of the Metropolitan Regional Committee

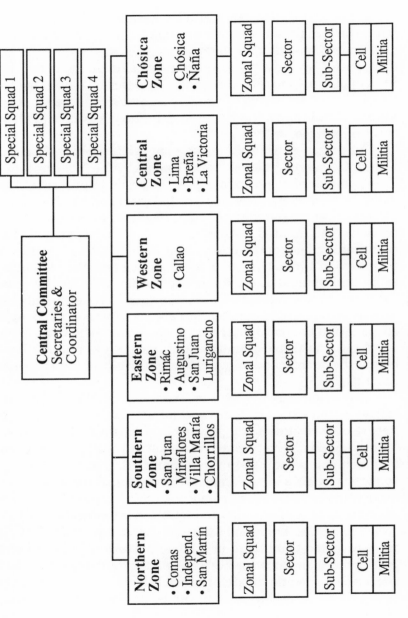

Source: Data from DIRCOTE, 1988, updated by the author.

60

civilians – a couple in love, street vendors, students, et cetera. Generally they do not carry visible arms or explosives; these are provided by "purveyors" at the moment of the attack (operating as separate entities, the purveyors do not work within any particular squad). The second special squad, the "assault group," signals the beginning of the action by creating a state of chaos in the immediate area of the attack. This assignment may involve throwing dynamite or homemade bombs. By creating confusion of this sort, the assault group opens an umbrella of commotion over the surrounding area, providing the annihilation detachment with a moment of cover in which to execute its attack. Once its duty has been accomplished, the assault group melts back into the street, generally into getaway cars or into the crowds.[5]

While the annihilation squad is carrying out its strike, the third special squad, the "containment detachment," steps in to neutralize any counterattack. Finally, the fourth squad or "razing detachment" will appear climactically, culminate the attack – for example, by delivering a final shot to the head or chest in the case of an assassination – and leave a placard claiming the attack for Sendero Luminoso. The fourth squad is often composed of a single individual – in many cases, a woman. Attack sequences in Lima may occasionally differ from this pattern, but mostly follow this design with a disarming degree of efficiency.

Besides coordinating special squad assaults, the Sendero's Metropolitan Central Committee also programs Lima's six zonal committees and their four subsidiary divisions: zonal squads, sectors, subsectors, and cell militias. The responsibilities of each subdivision are not as explicitly defined as those of the special squads; instead, they serve in a variety of capacities. The zonal committees and their subdivisions are chiefly involved with the dissemination of Sendero ideology (that is, popular education) and the procurement of all categories of assistance for militants and other party members. The cell militia found in each metropolitan zone provides military support and backup for Sendero militants instigating offensive maneuvers within its geographic locale.

Support Organizations

The Sendero movement is further bolstered in Lima by a full array of support organizations. These groups are organized by Sendero to target and recruit all categories of city residents. Adopting the goals of different subgroups as its own, Sendero is able to attract and indoctrinate new party members and sympathizers. Once new supporters have been enlisted, their mission is twofold: first, to participate in agitation and propaganda and, second, to provide any and all possible support to the movement. A number of organizations fall into this category:

- Laborers and Workers' Class Movement (Movimiento Obrero de Trabajadores Clasistas or MOTC)
- Popular Peasants' Movement (Movimiento Campesino Popular or MCP)
- Shanty Town Movement (Movimiento de Pueblos Jovenes or MPJ)
- Mariátegui Center for Intellectual Work (Centro de Trabajo Intelectual Mariátegui or CTIM)
- Popular Bases Movement (Movimiento de Bases Populares or MBP)
- Women's Popular Movement (Movimiento Femenino Popular or MFP)
- Agricultural Laborers and Workers' Movement (Movimiento de Obreros y Trabajadores Agrícolas or MOTAG)
- Shanty Town Revolutionary Movement (Movimiento Revolucionario de Pueblos Jovenes or MRPJ)[6]

All of these organizations are believed to be grouped under the general title, People's Revolutionary Defense Movement (Movimiento Revolucionario de Defensa del Pueblo or MRDP).[7]

By far the most important of the grassroots movements, however, is Popular Aid of Peru (Socorro Popular del Peru), which was discovered by the police in January 1988. Under this single broad heading fall a number of smaller support groups that provide multiple categories of assistance and service to the insurgency and those associated with it. Founded in 1982, the organization furnishes medical, legal, and other professional advice to the movement as well as assisting with the acquisition of funds, transportation, food, and housing.

Authorities first became aware of Socorro Popular in late 1987 when a number of highly classified documents were captured from the apartment of a suspected Sendero commander, Roger Valle Travesano. These documents disclosed that Valle Travesano, an attorney, was a member of the Association of Democratic Lawyers, an organization that provides free legal aid to people arrested on charges of terrorism. The documents also revealed Socorro Popular's history of and potential for growth: from 1982 to 1986 the movement's membership expanded from 72 to some 600 members. This number has unquestionably grown since 1986, as university students from all over Peru, recruited while still studying, have graduated and put their professional skills to work for the insurgency. The current number of participants, therefore, is extremely difficult to determine.

The assistance program follows a specific pilot plan and time line that coordinates its activities with those of the insurgency. According to Valle Travesano's documents, as of August 1985, Socorro Popular was to take part in recruiting and organizing the masses on a national level, in part by promoting demonstrations and similar nonlethal exercises. Aside from Lima, the geographic areas to which the organization has been assigned are not areas of high Sendero activity but rather new, "unexposed" parts of the country such as Huaraz (as of 1986), Chimbote, and Ica. This tactic clears the path for the more traditional Sendero method of penetration – that is, popular education.

According to the organizational chart that DIRCOTE has formulated for Socorro Popular (see figure 5), the association is directed by a committee of approximately six members. Reporting directly to this body is the "Commission for Propaganda and Public Relations," a group that works with intellectuals to develop mass propaganda for Sendero. Beyond this commission, Socorro Popular is divided into three principal branches: the Department of Mobilization, the Department of Legal Defense, and the Department of Assistance.

Of the three subsections, the Department of Mobilization is the largest. Essentially, it is charged with two tasks: mobilizing and coordinating the masses in legal support of Sendero and assisting prisoners and their families. The former is accomplished with the help of existing groups such as the Revolutionary People's Movement and other organizations well integrated with the populace. The second assignment, carried out by the Prisoners' Aid Committee, is more unique and reveals the true depth of Sendero Luminoso's functional organization; its primary goal is to provide aid of all sorts to incarcerated militants and their families. Such support may be as simple as ensuring that the families of jailed or missing Senderistas have food and clothing or as complicated as pressing through legal channels for prisoner visitation rights or for disclosure of disappeared activists' whereabouts. In addition to these services, there is a subcommittee that tends the needs of the families of "fallen heroes" — Senderistas killed in action. Each of these groups is also charged with continuing education and indoctrination efforts at all times — a propitious method of reassuring those who are suffering that their pain is for a good cause. Here again, Sendero's attention to the feelings and sensitivities of its supporters is striking.

The Department of Legal Defense, as the name implies, is primarily responsible for the legal defense of Senderistas. The department has three divisions. The Association of Democratic Lawyers provides free legal services to detainees of terrorism; the Section of Law Students also pro-

FIGURE 5
Organization of Soccoro Popular

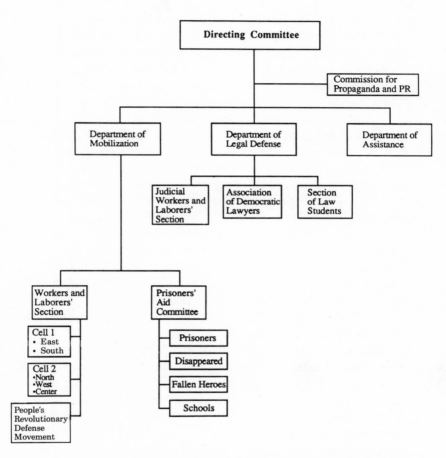

Source: "El Socorro de Sendero," *Caretas*, January 11, 1988, p. 64 (revised and updated with data provided by DIRCOTE).

vides free legal advice and works to cultivate interest in Sendero among other law students; and the Organization of Lay Workers presumably is composed of court system personnel—clerks, messengers, and secretaries. This latter group serves the insurgency by furnishing confidential information regarding prosecution plans in progress, by causing "accidental" delays within prosecution proceedings, and even by "misplacing" or "losing" important files.

The remaining division of Socorro Popular is known as "Assistance"—a vague title, but one that nevertheless describes the fundamental nature of the department. "Assistance" is made up of people who sympathize with Sendero but who are more useful to the movement in their present occupations than as full-time militants. These individuals are employed in nearly every area of the public and private sectors. There are electrical engineers, for example, who supply information about key sections of a region's electrical grid, sections that, if downed, will cut power from the greatest geographical areas; structural engineers who advise Senderistas of where to place explosives to make a bridge or building collapse; and any number of security officials who allow Senderistas admittance to sensitive areas. A particularly chilling case in which an "Assistance" member provided classified information to the insurgency is that of Eva Gómez, a National Police Hospital psychologist. Gómez, who graduated from the Catholic University (one of Peru's finest), worked in psychological evaluation of police officers who were sent to work in emergency zones. In this post she had access to extensive confidential records, including the backgrounds of police officers and their families, that she presumably passed on to key Sendero personnel. She was arrested in late 1987 by DIRCOTE.[8]

Ironically, those participating in Socorro Popular enterprises could not be prosecuted because membership in a nonmilitary political organization was not interpreted as constituting a crime. A Lima judge ruled in 1987 that prosecuting citizens for partaking in such activities would violate their constitutional rights. This area of legal interpretation has resulted in much controversy.

Hierarchy

Much like other military organizations, Sendero Luminoso is structured hierarchically, in five basic levels (see figure 6). The large foundation of the Sendero pyramid is composed of a nationwide body of "sympathizers." Individuals in this category have begun to develop an interest in the ideology of the movement and have agreed to take part in demonstrations and provide support in the form of money, medicine, clothes, arms, explosives, and certain services. Although sympathizers rarely participate in armed initiatives, they may store arms or deliver messages for those who do.

"Activists," mainly students, workers, and members of the urban and rural underclasses, constitute the next level of the Sendero organization. Although more involved than sympathizers, most activists have not yet committed themselves irreversibly to the movement (few resign after participating at the activist level, however). Activists' responsibilities include programming popular education, distributing leaflets and flyers, mobilizing the masses for demonstrations, organizing indoctrination, and, in general, spreading civil unrest in any way possible. Although not personally armed in these activities, they may often be accompanied by others who are.

The true military component of Sendero Luminoso begins at the "militant" level, the next tier on the structural pyramid. Militants compose the popular guerrilla army and are directly involved in all types of violent undertakings. Anyone at this stage within the organization must have demonstrated verifiable commitment to the insurgency, often by participating in a terrorist act or a similarly violent, life-threatening ordeal. Such commitment has made Sen-

FIGURE 6
Structure of Sendero Luminoso

1. PCP-SL Central Committee (the "cupola")
   - composed of Guzmán and his top lieutenants
   - directs the entire organization

2. Commanders
   - assigned by region
   - responsible for all political and military activity in their zone

3. Militants
   - compose the Popular Guerrilla Army
   - demonstrate unusually high commitment
   - involved in all types of violent action

4. Activists
   - composed of students, workers, and members of the urban and rural underclasses
   - educate and mobilize the masses (organize propaganda, spread leaflets and flyers)

5. Sympathizers
   - interested in the movement's ideology
   - take part in demonstrations
   - provide support (money, medicine, clothes, arms, explosives, and some services)

Note: Levels 1, 2, and 3 constitute the military portion of Sendero.

dero Luminoso extremely difficult for the armed forces or police to infiltrate.

Militants have pledged themselves to the insurgency, confident that Sendero's ultimate success is of far greater importance than even their own lives. "The life of an individual is worth nothing," explains an imprisoned Sendero soldier. "It's the masses that are important. When revolutionary blood is spilled, it is not in vain. That blood will fertilize new lives of combat for the revolution."[9]

Sendero's militants are directed, as in any military organization, by commanders (*mandos*). Assigned by geographic zone and sector, commanders are responsible for all the military and political activity in their region. To this end, most have a political chief and a military chief working directly beneath them. The men and women classified as militants and commanders are among the most ideologically committed in the entire organization. Their unusual degree of personal obligation – even fanaticism – strengthens the insurrection. Unlike the soldiers (many of whom are drafted) who make up the government's military forces, Sendero militants and commanders are fighting for ideological principles and the belief that Peru can have a better future through Sendero Luminoso. In short, they believe that they are fighting for themselves, their families, and their children.

At the top of the Sendero Luminoso structural pyramid is the National Central Committee or cupola. This group contains only a handful of people – the most elite members of the Sendero Luminoso organization, most of whom have participated in the movement since its inception at UNSCH in the mid-1960s and 1970s. The cupola directs all nationwide Sendero activities and advises regional commanders of policy changes and upcoming offensives. National Central Committee members also make all ideological and strategical policy decisions for the insurgency; in essence, they are the intellectual work force of the entire operation. The cupola works in absolute secrecy. Only minutes and records captured on rare occasions have offered any insight into the committee's operating procedures and membership. Most Peruvian scholars of Sendero believe that the cupola (among others) is made up of Abimael Guzmán, Osmán Morote (captured in 1988), Julio César Mezzich, Maximiliano Durant Araujo (currently residing in France), and Hildebrando Pérez.[10] The secretaries of the Metropolitan Central Committee are also members of the cupola, but their actual identities are currently unknown.[11] Some of the cupola members will be examined briefly here.

Osmán Morote

As a founder of the movement and a member of the National Central Committee, Osmán Morote was believed by many to be Sendero's second-in-command before his capture in 1988. Little is known about Morote's personal life before he became a student at UNSCH, where his father, Osmán Morote Best, was president. As a student of Guzmán's, the younger Morote took quickly to Communist doctrine and became known as a campus political activist. Among other student accomplishments, Morote was responsible for much of the FER cell activity at the university and for actually helping Guzmán found the PCP-SL when the PCP split in 1970.[12] Morote joined the faculty at Huamanga after a trip to China in 1975.

Until his capture in June 1988, Morote was believed by many to have been the organizational and military chief of the Sendero movement. He is attributed with forming Sendero's first military school, Inicio de la Lucha Armada 80 ("initiation of the armed struggle 80" or ILA 80), after which he went permanently underground. Police sources indicate that Morote was the commander of the movement's Principal Region (Ayacucho, Huancavelica, and Apurímac) until 1984. At that time he left to open the Northeastern Regional Front in the Upper Huallaga Valley, a brilliant strategical move that eventually led to Sendero's partnership with the cash and arms-rich cocaine traffickers. Once this front was able to stand on its own, Morote moved on to create Sendero's Northern Regional Zone in the departments of Cajamarca and La Libertad. (These departments are of tremendous tactical importance because, once captured, they permit easy mobilization of Sendero militants along the so-called northern Andean corridor.) As of early 1990, Morote was undergoing prosecution in Lima.

Julio César Mezzich

A top-notch organizer, Mezzich is known to be a member of the Sendero Luminoso National Central Committee. He was born into a middle-class Limeño family and attended one of the nation's finest private secondary schools, the Jesuit La Imaculada. His former classmates are now among the elite in Peruvian society, including diplomats, businessmen, doctors, lawyers, and members of the government. Well known for his exceptional athletic ability, Mezzich graduated in 1963 and went on to study at the University of Cayetano Heredia. There he became a militant in the leftist organization Vanguardia Revolucionaria and developed a deep interest in the Indian population of Peru. This concern eventually became so strong that Mezzich renounced the urban way of life and adopted that of his Andean friends. Working independently, he organized peasant movements in Andahuaylas and Apurímac before joining Guzmán and Sendero Luminoso in the mid-1970s.

Mezzich has not been seen in public since the movement went underground, and some presume that he is dead. Security forces affirm that Mezzich is among the most powerful members of the insurgency and that he could eventually replace Guzmán as director of the party. The police reward offered for his capture equals that offered for Guzmán.

Maximiliano Durant Araujo

As a professor of physics at the University of San Cristóbal, Durant was one of the original founders of Sendero

Luminoso. No data is available on his personal life before then. In 1982, he was released from prison where he was being held on charges of terrorism. Since that time he has lived in Paris, where he is believed to direct a group sympathetic to Sendero's cause under the auspices of the International Revolutionary Movement and the University of Paris. This organization arranges seminars about the insurgency and conducts fund-raising activities, such as selling posters that depict President Gonzalo and the call for armed struggle. Working in coordination with other proponents of Sendero Luminoso in Europe, he may also be involved in fundraising on a larger scale. Because Durant has been an expatriate for several years, his immediate role in the Sendero hierarchy is unknown. His image in French intellectual circles appears to be strong, however, and he is widely respected in France for his expertise in the field of energy. Both the Center for Scientific Investigation and the Commission of Atomic Energy in France have commended his scientific work.[13]

There are two other significant Senderistas whose mention should yield insight into the character of Sendero. Laura Zambrano Padilla and Teresa Angelica Cárdenas López are both former secretaries of the Metropolitan Regional Committee and members of the cupola.

Laura Zambrano Padilla

Known to others in the movement as "Meche," Zambrano was captured in 1984 and subsequently released for lack of evidence. While she was in captivity, leaflets appealing for her physical safety and discharge were widely distributed by the PCP in Lima. The flyers read "Let's save Meche," and threatened the police, judicial authorities, and their families if she were harmed.[14] Some have theorized that her release may have partly stemmed from these threats. Zambrano has been arrested subsequently on additional charges and is currently incarcerated in Lima.[15]

Teresa Angelica Cárdenas López

Educated as an anthropologist, Cárdenas (alias "Techi"), was unable to find formal employment after graduating. Poverty led her to work as a street vendor; frustration with the system led her to join Sendero Luminoso. She was captured by the Lima police in July 1983.

Techi's situation is typical of many upper-level Sendero militants. In spite of studies in Peru's university system, she found no opportunity for appropriate employment after graduating. Thus Techi, and many others like her, became distraught and disillusioned.

For thousands of men and women whose situation is similar, the alternative is to change the existing system. To accomplish this goal—in a radical way—they dedicate themselves to Sendero Luminoso.

Ability to Generate Leadership

One of the organizational factors that has made the Sendero Luminoso movement especially resilient is its ability to generate and regenerate leadership continuously. In spite of the Peruvian government's claim that many key Sendero leaders have been killed or imprisoned, the movement continues to grow in strength and dispersion. This degree of expansion suggests that Sendero has a standing cadre of skilled, available militants ready and able to step into leadership positions as needed. One example in particular illustrates this fact: in 1986, a large number of known commanders and high-level militants were being held in the Lurigancho and El Frontón prisons, and some experts hypothesized that the insurgency was in fact being directed by those in captivity. After a massive prison uprising in which some 256 Senderistas were killed, including a significant percentage of the directorship, the government believed that the insurgency might disintegrate. Obviously, this has not been the case. Although Sendero may have been wounded by the sudden, sweeping elimination of key leaders, the movement has nonetheless demonstrated that it does indeed have the ability to move new talent swiftly into suddenly vacated positions and continue its advances. After studying and combating the insurgency for eight years, police have concluded that Sendero leadership is by no means limited to a few individuals, but is rather the concerted effort of a well-oiled organizational structure in which trained, capable individuals are continuously accessible.

This ready supply of militants to whom a leadership position can be assigned at a moment's notice is largely a function of Sendero's tiered membership structure. Before an individual can achieve militant status (the grade from which new commanders are taken), he must prove his worth and commitment to the movement by serving first as a sympathizer and then as an activist. At each of these stages, every recruit must undergo rigorous indoctrinational training, which gives all Senderistas valuable hands-on experience and a more profound understanding of the movement itself. One of the primary goals of this system is to increase individual self-esteem, a characteristic often lacking among members of the Peruvian underclass. By assigning specific tasks to individuals and groups, Sendero is able to reinforce self-worth, encourage a coordinated work ethic, and foster a literally "spiritual" attachment to the party. In a country such as Peru, where opportunity and social mobility are both virtually nonexistent, Sendero can give people—youth especially—a sense of purpose and the self-esteem and pride to accompany it. By the time one is given a managerial role, he or she will be intensely attached to the movement in a passionate bond that bypasses personal interest and might easily be considered fanaticism. Not coincidentally, such individuals also will be highly familiar with the organization and its basic operating procedures. Through this system, Sendero guarantees itself well-trained leaders with an unusually profound level of personal commitment to the success of the movement.

Portrait of a Senderista

The basic requirement for interest in the Sendero Luminoso movement is very straightforward: the belief that one's personal situation offers little or no hope for social or economic mobility. This sentiment and the frustration and anxiety it creates are shared by millions of Peruvians. Most blame the government for their problems. For increasing numbers of frustrated people, Sendero Luminoso, whose widely publicized goal is destruction of the existing state, is the answer.

On a more personal level, members of this organization, like members of many terrorist and insurgent movements, may also be characterized by introverted personalities. These people are easily seduced by the trust, self-importance, and single-minded pursuit of a goal that participation in a movement such as Sendero Luminoso may cultivate. Many Peruvian students are also, by the nature of their situation, attracted to Sendero. After laboring diligently in Peru's demanding universities to earn degrees, many are unable to find employment commensurate with their education or ability. Frustrated by the system and its notable lack of opportunity, they turn to Sendero. Participating in the movement gives these people a sense of purpose and hope for the future that the incumbent system does not provide or seemingly even attempt to provide.

Sendero leaders, ever wary and analytical of the environments in which they are working, have recognized these traits and have directed their recruiting efforts accordingly. They solicit heavily among both students and the financially prostrate rural and urban underclasses. The lumpen intelligentsia, a class that throughout Peru feels trapped in its social and economic setting, is also an appealing target. Reliable, capable, intelligent, and committed, these people make excellent members and supporters for the movement.

Sendero has most recently turned its attention to the tremendous potential for securing support among the masses of people migrating to Lima from Peru's depressed countryside. As their meager savings disappear and the difficulty of obtaining employment begins to bear down heavily upon them and their families, Sendero's rhetorical promises of a better future become progressively more alluring.

Women

The Sendero Luminoso movement is also incrementally strengthened by a heavy emphasis on female membership. Women have historically played a leading role in the insurrection, a calling that has given them a new importance in Peruvian history. Like most Latin American cultures, Peruvian society is still largely dominated by machismo. Although women do pursue higher education and prepare for independent lives, society and tradition continue to push them toward secondary, passive roles. Throughout Peru, women are strongly tied to keeping house, caring for men, and raising children. Those who do venture into the business world are generally found in secondary positions. In many cases, especially in the lower classes, women are economically deprived and physically abused. Sendero Luminoso offers liberation from the traditional familial and societal female roles by treating women and men equally. Hence, for the women fighting in Sendero's ranks, the struggle holds higher stakes than political and economic justice; for female Senderistas, it is a battle for gender equality.

Encouraging female participation in a revolutionary movement is not a new phenomenon. Lenin spoke of the importance of women's participation in the Russian Revolution. Mao devoted lengthy paragraphs to the condition of women in China. Mariátegui wrote of the significance of women's roles in Peruvian society in the late 1920s. And Guzmán has taken all three concepts and applied them to present-day Peru.

It is perhaps Mao's perception of women that is most relevant to the Peruvian situation. According to Mao, women in semifeudal and semicolonial societies suffer from four categories of oppression: political, societal, marital, and religious. The only way to liberate women from these historical roles and realize genuine equality between the sexes is through transforming the state to a socialist (that is, Communist) system.[16] Mariátegui concurs with this stance and states further that women, like men, belong to a social class and that their interests are those of their class before those of their sex. Guzmán has merged these concepts and instigated them as standard curricula in Sendero's popular schools. Female teachers in these schools explain that it is necessary for underclass women to be conscious of the double exploitation that they face — class and sex — and the importance of fighting for emancipation from both. True female liberation, they teach, will come with the destruction of private property and the class antagonism it generates. Only then will the traditional home economic situation that stupefies, oppresses, and removes women from the social struggle be eliminated.[17]

The Sendero Luminoso movement has begun the women's liberation process in ways immediately visible to its members. In addition to holding such administrative leadership roles as secretary of the Metropolitan Regional Committee, women receive many of Sendero's most cold-blooded terrorist and military assignments. The analysis of almost any major assassination usually reveals that a woman has been charged with delivering the lethal shot. Beyond ideology, Sendero's reason for assigning women missions of this type lies deep within the organization's structural design. Difficult, dangerous, and mentally demanding assignments give women a chance to prove themselves and to enhance their self-confidence. Moreover, such assignments prove to women themselves, as well as others, that they are indeed capable of maintaining leadership roles in the movement, and subsequently the new state. Finally, female participation in Sendero provides vindication for the centuries of submission that Latin American women have endured; it is their chance to strike back violently at the traditional system that oppresses them.[18]

5

Government Response

Laws to Combat Terrorism

During 1980–1981, Sendero Luminoso's first year of insurgent activity alone, the movement was responsible for 482 terrorist incidents.[1] Accordingly, the number of arrests and detentions of suspected terrorist offenders began to climb as well. But the rise of Sendero caught the Peruvian legal community off guard. As of 1980, the only existing laws applicable to terrorist trials (in addition to the other common crimes—homicide, bodily injury, and property damage—already in the Penal Code) were such legal categories of offense as "disturbance of internal peace," "disruption of public order," and "conspiracy to introduce political terrorism into the country."[2] Existing legislation nowhere provided for the criminal type of terrorism now being perpetrated by the insurgency. Members of the Peruvian legal profession, overwhelmed by the sheer numbers of terrorist cases, were now stumped by the ethical ambiguities of cases involving suspected Senderistas.

The government and its Ministry of Justice recognized the necessity of creating new legislation to handle Sendero-related trials more effectively. It must be remembered, however, that the conception and implementation of tough laws on terrorism were to transpire in the context of Peru's fledging democratic processes and institutions. After 11 years of dictatorial military rule, a new democratically elected Constitutional Convention promulgated Peru's Constitution on July 12, 1979.[3] This Constitution, which took effect the following year, enshrined fundamental rights and freedoms not guaranteed under military rule — freedom of expression, freedom of the press, and freedom of political association, among others.

The issue of creating legislation to prosecute perpetrators of insurgent activity raised ethical questions in the desire to uphold fully the rights and freedoms protected under the nation's new Constitution. In legal circles those concerned about observing the letter of the Constitution proposed trying suspected terrorists as common criminals subject to ordinary justice (*justicia ordinaria*). Others, however, viewed acts of terrorism as equal to acts of treason and maintained that special legislation was necessary to protect national security interests. Lawyers and legal officials subscribing to this school of thought held that proceedings for suspected terrorists should be conducted by military tribunals. The Peruvian government chose to categorize suspected terrorists as common criminals and thereby protect their constitutionally guaranteed rights.

On March 10, 1981, President Fernando Belaúnde promulgated the first law on terrorism, Legislative Decree 46.[4] To alleviate legal obstacles that had begun to surface in terrorist trials, this decree created a substantive law that recognized terrorism as a complex criminal act and defined it in comprehensive, more effective terms. The spirit of this substantive law was to protect the security and stability of the state in the face of a unique form of crime that was striking against the individual and collective interests of the community — life, health, and property.[5] This decree served both to place Peruvian society under this legal framework of protection and to provide a legal safeguard for the interests and institutions of the state. A translation of Article 1 of Legislative Decree 46 is as follows:

One who, with the intent to provoke or maintain a situation of alarm, apprehension, or terror in the population or in a sector of it, perpetrates acts which could create risk for the life, health, or property of the people, or is directed to the destruction or detriment of public or private buildings, roads or means of communication and transportation, or the conduction of fluids or motor forces or analogues, using means capable of producing great destruction, or occasioning great perturbation of public tranquility, or affecting adversely international relations, or undermining the security of the state will be penalized with a penitentiary sentence of not less than 10 years and not more than 20 years.[6]

In essence, then, Legislative Decree 46 introduced a terrorist typology into Peruvian ordinary legislation (*legislacion ordinaria*). Three elements of crime were stated: (1) the intent of the agent to create a situation of terror (a subjective element); (2) the agent's act of striking against life, health, property, and other protected individual and community interests (an objective element); and (3) the agent's means of wielding destruction—through the use of firearms, explosives, fire, inundation, et cetera (another objective element).[7] In addition to this rather generic description of criminal acts categorized as terrorism, it is crucial to highlight the decree's guidelines for specifying the circumstances in which an agent can be classified as a terrorist:

(a) By belonging to an organization or criminal gang of three or more people that employs terrorism as a tactic for the achievement of its goals, in the short- or the long-term, whatever these goals may be, an individual can be considered a terrorist solely because of his or her association with that entity.[8]

(b) By leading an organization or criminal gang of the type described previously, an individual can be considered a terrorist solely because of his or her leadership of that entity.[9]

(c) By inciting terrorism by use of the press, radio, television, or any other medium of mass communication so as to incite an indeterminate number of people to commit either of the acts (Art. 1) considered terrorism.[10]

(d) By expressing publicly apology for or praise of the act of terrorism already committed or apology for or praise of the individual found guilty as the author or accomplice of the act of terrorism.[11]

It should also be noted that, as mandated by Article 109 of the Constitution, terrorism is considered a common crime (*delito común*) rather than a political crime.[12] Thus, terrorists cannot benefit from special dispositions pertinent to political crimes such as extradition and asylum.

Controversy soon arose over the definition of terrorism embodied in Legislative Decree 46, with opponents denouncing the definition as dangerously broad. These critics argued that the new law infringed upon such constitutionally guaranteed rights as freedom of expression, political association, and dissemination of political propaganda. Despite such criticisms, the decree remained in effect for six years. Under the García administration, however, Congress enacted Law 24651 on March 19, 1987, and thereby ultimately revoked Legislative Decree 46. Although no expression of cause exists for this revocation, it is widely known in Peru that the creation of Law 24651 resulted from a far-reaching campaign, spearheaded in large measure by Marxist groups, launched ostensibly in defense of the constitutional freedoms mentioned above. As a result of Law 24651, the decree's four legal categories for terrorism (quoted above) were removed, and Peruvian society has thereby been deprived of the most effective legal instrument for social defense. With the passage of Law 24651, the leaders of Sendero Luminoso have been all but exempted from police and judiciary investigations.

In June 1987, Congress enacted yet another piece of terrorist legislation—Law 24700. This procedural law was an attempt to provide further protection for detainees by dictating that a prosecutor from the Public Ministry and a defense lawyer must be present at all stages of police investigation following an individual's apprehension.[13] In the interest of protecting national security, this law prohibits presentation of a petition of habeus corpus on behalf of the detainee for a period of 15 days after arrest.

Again, these new terrorist laws generated much controversy, this time in response to the apprehension of a key Senderista. In June 1988, Osmán Morote was captured in Lima. Under Law 24651, he was actually absolved of some of the crimes with which he was charged, although he remains in custody for others. Although Morote's positions as Sendero leader, member of the cupola, and the insurgency's commander of the northern region were well known by the police, the judges ruled that Morote's direct participation in Sendero activities — a matter of judgment — could not be proven beyond doubt. The internal documents of Sendero Luminoso found in Morote's possession, in his own handwriting, were insufficient to justify a pronouncement of guilt.[14] Morote remains in custody for other charges.

The ensuing public outcry over Morote's technical "innocence" pressed the government to pass yet another law pertaining to the legal treatment of terrorists. Enacted on December 7, 1988, Law 24953 served to revoke Law 24651 and attempted to improve upon it by reinstating three criminal categories of terrorist offenses:[15]

(a) Belonging to an organization of two or more individuals in an association resulting in the instigation, organization, dissemination, or planning, encouraging, or committing of acts of terrorism in either the short- or long-term.[16]

(b) Inciting of the public to commit acts of terrorism by use of the mass media.[17]

(c) Apologizing for or commending of or praising of an act of terrorism already perpetrated, or the praising of the agent or agents found guilty in a trial.[18]

Despite Morote's capture and unsuccessful trial, however, the government did not reinstate a provision that defines one as a terrorist solely for being the leader of a terrorist organization. Compared with Legislative Decree 46 and Law 24651, Law 24953 has increased the penalties associated with a conviction for terrorist activity, including a 25-year minimum prison term (see table 1).

Special Tribunals

Members of the legal establishment found themselves hard-pressed to mold terrorist-related proceedings to the extant modus operandi of the judicial system. In bringing cases to trial, they faced a two-fold challenge — effectively using the broad-based definition of terrorism mandated by Legislative Decree 46 and subsequent laws while upholding the rights and freedoms enshrined in the Constitution. The application of ordinary justice required under the Constitution proved largely ineffectual. The labyrinth of bureaucratic intricacies inherent in the system rendered the process of trial and conviction slow, lengthy, and often fruitless.

Conviction in the Peruvian court system requires proof beyond reasonable doubt that the suspect is responsible for the crimes with which he is charged. Because of the critical nature of the Sendero Luminoso threat, however, the police and army have exercised liberal arresting procedures that have clogged the courts with state cases against people whose only crime may have been their presence in an area where Sendero actions took place. Hundreds of suspected Senderistas and suspected Sendero sympathizers throughout the nation were sometimes incarcerated, often with little or no evidence to justify their arrest and detention. The overwhelming burden these accusations placed on the courts caused many cases against true Senderistas to be lost in the shuffle and countless others to be dismissed for lack of evidence.[19]

The continual release of suspected insurgency members caused a great deal of discord among the Peruvian police and the armed forces (both groups believed their efforts to apprehend terrorists were not rewarded with convictions), as well as the general populace. Initially, judicial officials attributed the problem to two causes. First, because little or no security was available to protect magistrates working in departments where Sendero was active, such officials were reluctant to indict rebels whose counterparts voiced constant threats. Second, few magistrates had actually been trained to take the bench in terrorist-related cases. In an attempt to combat these factors, Justice Minister Elias Larosa decreed in early 1982 that all terrorist cases were henceforth to be tried in Lima.[20] This radical step involved the physical transfer of hundreds of suspected terrorists from throughout the country to Lima, where they were detained in crowded, highly unsanitary prison facilities. Terrorist trials moved even more slowly than before, as mountains of paperwork were routed between provincial magistrates and Lima. Although intimidation against provincial magistrates was doubtless reduced, the sheer volume of terrorist cases proved too great for the already overworked Court of Lima. The judges were further hampered by the legal principle that, given insufficient or questionable evidence, rulings were to give the accused the benefit of the doubt. After four years, this law was revoked, and terrorist trials were subsequently resumed in the provinces by Law 24499 of April 22, 1986.

Still pursuing a method that would process terrorist cases more effectively, Peruvian legislators enacted a law in June 1987 that created Special Tribunals (*Tribunales Especiales*) dedicated exclusively to hearing cases on the insurgency.[21] Magistrates were appointed by the Supreme Court and the attorney general to staff the new courts at all stages, from the provincial to the national levels. Those appointed to serve in the Special Tribunals were granted a substantial pay increase and accrual time equal to twice that received for working in the regular court system. Despite these bonuses, many magistrates were disinclined to accept the new positions. Some maintained that the high level of inherent risk was not worth the extra compensation

TABLE 1
Legal Penalties for Terrorism

Offense	Legislative Decree 46	Law 24651	Law 24953
Terrorism (general)	Penitentiary term of no less than 10 years and no more than 20 years	Penitentiary term of no less than 15 years or *internamiento*	Penitentiary term of no less than 15 years
Organization or gang membership			
Affiliation	Penitentiary term of no less than 2 years and no more than 5 years	Not covered	Affiliation provision reinstated; penitentiary term of no less than 10 years and no more than 15 years
Action	Penitentiary term of no less than 12 years	Penitentiary term of no less than 18 years	Penitentiary term of no less than 10 years and no more than 18 years
Leader or head			
Affiliation	Penitentiary term of no less than 6 years and no more than 12 years solely for being a leader	Not covered	Mere leader not covered
Action			*Internamiento* if leader participates in overt action

Bodily injury	Penitentiary term of no less than 12 years	Penitentiary term of no less than 18 years	Penitentiary term of no less than 18 years
Using a minor in acts of terrorism	Penitentiary term of no less than 15 years	Penitentiary term of no less than 18 years	Penitentiary term of no less than 18 years
Damage to public or private property	Penitentiary term of no less than 15 years	Penitentiary term of no less than 18 years	Penitentiary term of no less than 20 years
Death or grave injury	Internamiento	Internamiento	Internamiento
Extortion or kidnapping/hijacking	Not covered	Penitentiary term of no less than 18 years	Internamiento
Inciting terrorism	Penitentiary term of no less than 4 years and no more than 8 years	Not covered	Penitentiary term of no less than 5 years
Apologism for terrorism	Penitentiary term of no less than 3 years and no more than 5 years	Not covered	Penitentiary term of no less than 5 years

Note: Internamiento is a substitute for the death penalty. It consists of a minimum prison sentence of 25 years and an undetermined maximum in solitary confinement (could be equivalent to life in prison). The death penalty does not exist in Peru. In practice, *internamiento* actually consists of serving one year in solitary confinement and the remaining time in the same facilities as regular prisoners (owing to the lack of Peruvian prison facilities).

The margin between the minimum and maximum time set forth in the law enables the judges to consider the objective and personal circumstances of the matter and apply penalities on an individual basis.

When, during the investigation and trial, the same agent is responsible for different crimes (crimes against life, against property, against public tranquility, against communications, against the security of the state; or crimes adversely affecting international relations), the penalty for the most serious charge will be applied in one trial and one sentence (for example, *internamiento* for a minimum of 25 years).

Source: Legislative Decree 46, Law 24651, and Law 24953, as compiled, analyzed, and interpreted by the author.

offered. A number even preferred resignation to sitting on a Special Tribunal.[22]

Nevertheless, the first Special Tribunal—a temporary one—began its duties in September 1987 in Lima, just four months after the law creating it had been passed. The court was criticized almost immediately within the judicial community for its hasty organization. The judges assigned to it faltered in their decision making, convinced that any rulings they made might endanger themselves and their families. The program proceeded as planned, however, and on January 1, 1988, XI Tribunal of Lima—created solely to hear terrorist cases—began its first official judicial year. Although strict verdicts were handed down by the new tribunal, these rulings quickly began to take their toll.[23] Threats from Senderistas increased, and the three judges and their assistants were exhausted by the seemingly endless flow of cases confronting them. According to judicial department statistics, the XI Tribunal of Lima was assigned some 250 cases involving nearly 300 suspected terrorists at the commencement of its duties.

By decision of the Supreme Court on March 8, 1988, the XI Tribunal of Lima was dissolved after only two months of its first official judicial year because cases continued to move slowly. The Supreme Court mandated that the 14 Criminal Tribunals of Lima take an equitable share of those cases.[24] In short, the Lima-based Special Tribunal system did not work. At present, Sendero-related cases are tried in criminal courts throughout the nation.

The only Special Tribunal now in existence is to address the trial of Osmán Morote and the burgeoning number of processes in which he is included. The Supreme Court had ordered that all Morote proceedings (which in 1989 were being conducted in three Criminal Tribunals) be merged into one proceeding by the end of 1989. It charged the Court of Lima to form a Special Tribunal for the sole purpose of judging Morote. The Court of Lima appointed three judges to this Special Tribunal. One of them requested exemption, alluding to health reasons that precluded his acceptance. (His request was denied.) Judicial insiders knew that all three judges asked for special securities and insurance as prerequisites for such a position—for example, high personal protection by trained antisubversive personnel, armored cars, and life insurance for at least $100,000.[25] The magistrates took office to judge Morote on June 13, 1989.[26] It is not known whether the government has acceded to the judges' petitions.

Counteroffensive Initiatives

The first major counteroffensive against Sendero Luminoso was initiated in June 1981 by the Belaúnde administration. It came in response to mounting evidence that the movement actually posed a serious threat to government authority in the south-central Andean region. Previously, the state had preferred to consider Sendero a mere regional conflict. The antisubversive operation was conducted by DIRCOTE, the newly formed counterterrorism division of the Peruvian Investigative Police (Policía de Investigaciones del Perú or PIP).[27] This police division was supported by two existing special force squads similar to U.S. SWAT teams—the Sinchis and the Llapan Aticcs (both named for legendary Inca warriors).[28] In spite of the large scope of the operation, police forces were seriously underequipped and undertrained. They lacked crucial tactical planning, logistical support, and communications systems. In fact, they did not even have radios. Shortly, it became apparent that the police forces would not be able to contain the insurgency on their own.

State of Emergency

The Peruvian Constitution allows a state of emergency to be declared when national security is threatened.[29] In such cases, constitutionally guaranteed personal rights (assembly, travel, and inviolability of residence) are suspended within the emergency zone. Security forces may therefore search and arrest without warrant. A senior army officer appointed by the president serves as the administrative, political, and military chief of the zone during the emergency period. The law requires that the court system continue to operate under the state of emergency, although judicial power and effectiveness are severely impaired by the Political and Military Command. (The respective jurisdictions of the judiciary and the Political and Military Command have not been defined clearly by law within emergency zone.)

On December 21, 1982, President Belaúnde and his cabinet approved Supreme Decree 068-82, which ordered the armed forces to take control of the Ayacucho/Apurímac region and restore order. The state of emergency was implemented in Ayacucho by a coordinated intervention of the army, the navy infantrymen, and the air force. The army provided the bulk of the manpower, and the air force arranged for troop transport, air cover, surveillance, and other logistical assistance. On the afternoon of December 23, 1982, three air force planes carrying 450 soldiers landed in Ayacucho.[30] These forces were to secure the provinces of Huamanga, Huanta, La Mar, Víctor Fajardo, and Cangallo in the department of Ayacucho; the province of Andahuaylas in Apurímac; and later the province of Angaraes in Huancavelica.[31] The emergency zone was placed under the Political and Military Command of Army General Clemente Noel Moral.

Within the zone, army and police detachments were sent to all towns and villages where Sendero was thought to be active. In each settlement's main plaza, the government forces reaffirmed state authority in solemn ceremonies by raising the Peruvian flag, singing the national anthem, and pledging allegiance. Unfortunately, these tactics failed to intimidate the insurgency; Sendero's regional attacks continued unabated. In fact, the movement even stepped up its military activity, provoking and harassing the state forces in every way possible.

Army officers and soldiers in turn were frustrated by

their complete inability to distinguish members of the insurgency from local inhabitants. Their rage was unleashed in largely futile attempts to strike back at the subversive movement. Their offensives, strewn with human rights abuses, attracted the attention of organizations such as Americas Watch and Amnesty International, who raised their voices in defense of human rights in Peru.[32] The military was accused of numerous crimes, including disappearances (unacknowledged detentions), torture, rape, aggravated homicide, extrajudicial executions, and even genocide.

International observers and their Peruvian counterparts charged that the military had grossly exceeded the limits of power extended to it under the state of emergency.[33] In 1983, there were 2,223 unnatural civilian deaths reported in the state-of-emergency area, a massive jump from 128 recorded in 1980–1982. In 1983, 1,398 were believed to be Senderistas, compared with 48 in 1982. The ratio of civilian to military and police deaths in the region is also wildly skewed: for every member of the government forces killed in 1983, an average of 37 civilian deaths occurred (including suspected Senderistas).[34] Certainly all of these casualties cannot be attributed to the military; they unquestionably resulted also from Sendero-initiated violence. Nevertheless, the radical surge in mortality during the first year of military intervention is indicative of the government forces' heavy reliance on violent tactics.

It was the August 1984 discovery of three mass graves in Ayacucho – all attributed to military action – that actually incited the greatest public outrage. An informant disclosed the existence of the graves to Attorney General Alvaro Rey de Castro, who immediately sent an emissary to the area to investigate. Fernando Olivera, secretary general of the National Attorney's office, reported that the three mass graves contained 50 blindfolded bodies, many with fractured skulls and limbs. The incident took place in Pucayacu, a small town in the province of Huanta. This area was under the control of the Marine Infantrymen (*Infantes de Marina*), a navy special forces unit not unlike the U.S. Navy's Seal Squad. Further investigations revealed that the *Infantes* were, in fact, responsible for the crime.

The government realized that military intervention alone would not solve the highland insurgency problem. In 1983, the same year the state of emergency took effect, President Belaúnde drafted an economic assistance plan for the region. This plan called for the state to inject roughly U.S. $28 million into the area for irrigation and development projects.[35] The president and his cabinet reasoned correctly that investment was a prerequisite if the allegiance of the local population were to be maintained.[36] Yet natural catastrophes (floods in the north of Peru, droughts in the south) coupled with the Belaúnde administration's gravest economic crisis ultimately precluded the plan's implementation.[37] Another factor influencing the abandonment of the regional economic assistance plan was the government's underestimation of the dimensions of the Sendero threat.

The state of emergency continued in 1984 under a newly appointed political and military chief, Army General Adrian Huamán Centeno. Fluent in Quechua (the native language of the region) and a mestizo himself, Huamán sympathized with the Indians and pressed openly for regional investment and socioeconomic reforms. He clearly intended to reform the counterinsurgency strategy, stressing the importance of combining economic assistance with military presence. The central government was not pleased by the general's willingness to vent his dissatisfaction to the media, however, and Huamán was removed from his post by the end of the year.

During 1985, the highlands' counterinsurgency program was divided into two segments as a result of that year's presidential election. From January until July, government action in the area continued without major modification under the direction of Army General Wilfredo Mori. During this period the insurgency was extremely active, killing peasants in reprisal for aiding the military and the police. The government forces, in turn, responded by entering towns and shooting anyone suspected of being a Sendero sympathizer. Between the two, death tolls continued to escalate.

When power transferred to the García administration on July 28, 1985, the change was apparent almost immediately in the emergency zone. Before taking office, the commission formulating García's government plan (CONAPLAN) was instructed to design a more effective counterinsurgency strategy.[38] The plan recommended a "pacification drive," including emergency economic assistance, selective amnesty for adults associated with the insurgency, and pardon for minors. It also called for dialogues to be held with the Sendero Luminoso leadership. But Sendero was indignantly opposed to the suggested dialogues, and the remainder of the plan was ultimately shelved. The suggestion for desperately needed economic assistance was never implemented in a comprehensive manner. The discovery of another mass grave, however, enabled the new administration to demonstrate its counterinsurgency procedures.

Upon learning of the new grave's existence, President Alan García informed the Joint Chiefs of Staff that they had 72 hours to prepare a report on the issue and present it to the Congress. Never before in Peruvian history had a civilian president given such an imperious order to the nation's military establishment. General Sinesio Jarama, chairman of the Joint Chiefs, and General Wilfredo Mori, political and military chief of the emergency zone, delivered their findings to a special Senate subcommittee on September 16, 1985. Jarama explained that government forces operations had been carried out near the Ayacucho town of Accomarca between August 13 and August 15. During this time, there were three reports of combat between the military patrols and subversives; 46 civilians were killed, all reportedly Sendero sympathizers. Simultaneously, in Ayacucho an army lieutenant admitted to the local army command that he was responsible for the killings. As a result, both Jarama and Mori were dismissed from their posts, and the lieutenant, Telmo Hurtado Hurtado, was placed in custody and later tried in military court.[39]

This course of events also led to the temporary deactivation of almost all military operations in the emergency zone. Army patrols were reduced and detachments were pulled back from remote sectors of the countryside. Officers and troops were told not to act before new orders were issued. The inhabitants of the Ayacucho region were left to defend themselves with peasant patrols. Sendero took advantage of the lull in military activity to sack the villages that had cooperated with government forces.[40] Military operations in the highlands were resumed shortly, and with them resumed reports of human rights violations. Debate continues in Congress over the validity of a law requiring that military personnel accused of committing abuses be tried in civil, rather than military, courts. In 1988, 36 provinces in 7 of Peru's 24 departments were under a state of emergency. By late 1989, one third of Peru was under a state of emergency.[41]

Peasant Patrols

Peasant patrols (*rondas campesinas*) are an indigenous method of self-defense used by rural communities in the Andean highlands.[42] During the late 1970s, the system was revived in the northern Andean department of Cajamarca. Residents of the town of Cuyumalco spontaneously organized a team of local men to protect their livestock and property against thieves because the area's police were notoriously ineffective. This problem was not unique to Cuyumalco, and the idea soon spread to other regions of the department. Small towns banded together and formed common peasant patrols to police their territories. When a thief was apprehended, he was either informally sentenced by the patrols themselves or handed over to the authorities. From Cajamarca, the idea of the peasant patrol spread to the neighboring department of Piura. Thus the patrols confronted problems that were of interest and importance to all of the involved communities.[43]

When government forces took military and political control of the provinces of Huamanga, Huanta, La Mar, Víctor Fajardo, and Cangallo in Ayacucho, it was decided that a similar peasant patrol system should be implemented there to combat the insurgency. The military believed that the presence of such patrols would inhibit open Senderista activity in the area as well as provide the townspeople with a method of defending themselves in the absence of the army or the police. By military authority, the army literally picked up and clumped together whole villages of indigenous inhabitants, with the reasoning that it would be easier for both the peasant patrols and the military to protect settlements that were less geographically diffuse. In a sense, this strategy was very similar to the pacification program applied by the United States in Vietnam and the model village (*aldea modelo*) initiative implemented in Guatemala in 1982. The newly formed communities, known as Civil Defense Committees (*Comités de Defensa Civil*), were all placed under the formal jurisdiction of the emergency Political and Military Command.[44] A similar tactic was used in Peru in the latter half of the sixteenth century during the viceroyalty of Francisco de Toledo. The viceroy also hoped to achieve better control of the Indian settlements through the program, then known as *reducciones* (reductions).[45]

Not surprisingly, serious obstacles arose when the government-ordered Civil Defense Committee program began. Most of the Indian groups had not moved from their native territories in generations and were predictably hostile to the government's demand that they leave instantaneously. Conversely, those who suddenly found that they were expected to share their land with strangers from other communities reacted with equal indignation. The army also blundered by forcing unfriendly groups to unite in individual Civil Defense Committees. Carlos Iván Degregori, an expert on

the Sendero phenomenon, has pointed out that these re-
actions partially resulted from the heterogeneous and highly fragmented nature of Ayacucho's rural population.[46] The
government initiative aggravated age-old rivalries deeply
embedded in the region's varied ethnic makeup.

One of the towns chosen by the military to become a
Civil Defense Committee was Chuchi—the settlement from
which Sendero had launched its armed struggle in 1980 by
burning presidential ballot boxes. The inhabitants of Quis-
pillacta, a village long at odds with Chuchi over a land
dispute, were ordered to move to Chuchi in mid-1983 as part
of the new peasant patrol program. This attempt at over-
night cohabitation proved disastrous.[47] Instead of combating Sendero or protecting their combined interests, the two
groups bitterly fought each other. This situation was not
unique: throughout Ayacucho, when heterogeneous Indian
groups were forced to live together in Civil Defense Committee settlements, peasants violently confronted other
peasants. Not fully comprehending the situation, inhabitants of native villages ironically began to think that membership in the Sendero movement signified only that they
were opposed to leaving their native lands and joining a
Civil Defense Committee.

The few successfully united Civil Defense Committees
were neither prepared to combat the insurgency nor to
defend themselves against it. Armed only with knives,
clubs, and occasionally a single gun, they were ill-equipped
to face the brutal Sendero terrorists. Despite the nature
of their plight, the Indian communities had little choice
but to submit to the government's demands to form peasant patrols: to do otherwise was tantamount to confessing
allegiance to the insurgency, which would mean certain military reprisal. Towns suspected of assisting the movement
were immediately and violently entered. In these cases, the
soldiers, frustrated by their inability to distinguish between townspeople and Senderistas, shot people indiscriminately. White flags signifying functional Civil Defense
Committees therefore appeared throughout rural Ayacucho.

Unfortunately, these white flags quickly became targets for the insurgency.

Sendero attacked the new settlements with a vengeance, particularly those housing groups that had supported the insurgency before joining the Civil Defense initiative. Among the more bloody examples of Sendero's reprisals is the case of Rumi Rumi. The insurgency occupied the town in December 1987 and forced town leaders and male youths into a schoolhouse. There, they were beaten, shot, and hacked to death.[48] Similar cases abound. The growing frequency of such violent incidents is paralleled by heightened paranoia among government personnel in the area. No longer is it sufficient for Indians to swear allegiance to the government and form a Civil Defense Committee; peasant patrols are now virtually required to apprehend insurgents to prove their loyalty. Caught in the cross fire, the Andean communities are literally being bled to death.

Those living in the Civil Defense Committees also endure extreme hardships completely unrelated to the ubiquitous violence. With the populations of up to four towns concentrated in a single area, living conditions have become nearly unbearable. Disease is rampant, malnutrition widespread. Those who have been displaced have no land. Trained as farmers, few have been able to secure another source of income. They live under tremendous psychological stress and are materially in dire need. As the adult male populations of these settlements dwindle, women and even children have been forced to serve in the peasant patrols. Many families have fled the area, adding to the ever-expanding shanty towns that surround Lima and other large cities. Many more would like to flee, but have neither the resources nor the strength to do so.

Seven years after implementation (1983–1989), the Civil Defense Committees have served only to pit Peruvians against Peruvians. Compelled to fight a war without victors, the indigenous population, which Sendero claims to represent, is the true victim of Sendero Luminoso's revolution and the government's ineffectiveness.[49]

By the end of 1989, only one area in Peru seemed to have a successful peasant patrol. It is located in the rain forest of the department of Ayacucho, province of La Mar, and groups 85 indigenous communities. Its leader is Pompeyo Rivera Torres, known by his *nom de guerre* "Huayhuaco." In late 1989, President García gave the members of the peasant patrol 200 hunting guns to use in defending themselves.[50]

6

Narcoterrorism

This chapter is a case study of how Sendero Luminoso has entered the Upper Huallaga Valley, adapted itself to local conditions, and capitalized upon the area's resources. Sendero's wresting of the Upper Huallaga away from government control and its remarkable permeation of the hearts and minds of the valley's inhabitants provide a picture of what the future may hold for the rest of Peru unless the insurgency is effectively countered.

This case study describes the union of Sendero terrorists with the Upper Huallaga's flourishing coca-leaf and cocaine-paste industry, a phenomenon that has been dubbed "narcoterrorism." This marriage of convenience between drug producers and a terrorist insurgent group is not a phenomenon unique to Peru. The threat of narcoterrorism first surfaced in 1985 in Colombia when the Medellín drug cartel combined forces with a terrorist group, M-19, to attack the Supreme Court building in Bogotá to stop the extradiction of several drug kingpins.[1] This attack resulted in the assassination of 11 Supreme Court justices. Since this unprecedented tragedy, narcoterrorism has appeared in all coca and cocaine-producing countries in South America.

With their tremendous financial resources, profiteering narcotics cartels provide modern weaponry and funds to ideologically driven insurgents.[2] The combination of terrorist tactics and drug money has permeated the fabric of Latin American society because of the keen interest the terrorists and the drug-producing organizations share in destabilizing governments and in breaking down the established social order.[3] Although each side ultimately seeks different ends, in the short term each benefits from the association. Narcotics traffickers have adopted terrorist tactics to maintain the flow of drugs, acting with their own paramilitary forces and hired terrorists. The terrorists in turn have used drug money to fund insurgent activities aimed at the overthrow of Latin American governments and the restructuring of society along Marxist lines.

Peru's Upper Huallaga Valley is now home to what is indisputably Latin America's strongest narcoterrorist alliance. More coca is grown in the Upper Huallaga than anywhere else in the world, and the valley is a haven for numerous cocaine-paste manufacturing centers. Sendero Luminoso has penetrated the Upper Huallaga region of Peru, forging a monopoly of alliances with coca growers, cocaine-paste producers, and drug traffickers.[4] Aware of the benefits to be gained from cooperation, the coca and cocaine-paste producers and Sendero have formed a business relationship in which each side uses the other to achieve its respective goals. This chapter analyzes the nature of the region's inhabitants and socioeconomic characteristics, as well as Sendero's methods of penetrating and subduing the region. It also discusses the government's counterinitiatives.

Background of the Upper Huallaga Valley

The Upper Huallaga Valley is located on the eastern slopes of the northeastern Peruvian Andes at altitudes ranging approximately 1,500 to 6,000 feet above sea level. The region is referred to as Selva Alta in Peru. Endowed with rich vegetation, the area has been courted for its colonization potential since the Spanish conquest. During the sixteenth century, numerous missions departed to settle in the Upper Huallaga, but the rain-forest environment and extremely difficult conditions for travel and communications led to the abandonment of these early enterprises. Not until the early twentieth century did the region finally begin to realize some economic success. The *caucho* (rubber) boom that temporarily lifted the entire Amazon basin to world attention carried the Upper Huallaga Valley as well. Crude rubber extracted from rain-forest plants brought a startling amount of capital to the region, but failed to bring development. Moreover, because the rubber trade was conducted exclusively on the Amazon River system and used its Brazilian Atlantic ports, the valley did not become economically integrated with the rest of Peru, whose trade was routed through the Pacific coast.

The first real roads into the upper rain forest were completed in the 1940s, and migrants soon followed.[5] Most were Indian peasants fleeing from the acute agrarian problems wrought by the haciendas in the Andean highlands. Immigrant families formed spontaneous settlements in the Upper Huallaga Valley and surrounding areas. In addition to the small landholders, large tea and coffee plantations soon appeared in the region. The demand for labor on these estates attracted yet another wave of settlers to the Upper Huallaga. On occasions when the plantation owners were unable to summon a sufficient number of workers for planting or harvesting, emissaries would be sent to neighboring regions to contract peasants under the so-called *enganche* system.[6] When the need for labor subsided, many of the workers stayed in the area, establishing themselves as colonists.

It was not until the 1960s that the state began to play a significant role in colonizing the valley. Under President Fernando Belaúnde (1963–1968), the region was viewed anew as a source of rich natural resources and a possible solution to Peru's greatest demographic problem—the urban migration that was flooding the country's major cities.

Following a vision outlined in Belaúnde's book, *The Conquest of Peru by Peruvians* (Lima: Ediciones Tawantinsuyo, 1959), the state began to organize settlement projects, promoting the region as a land of plenty that held richness for all Peruvian citizens. In the early 1960s, the government began construction of the "Marginal Highway," which was to begin the process of developing the largely untouched South American interior. Thousands of impoverished city dwellers and highland peasants began the exodus to Peru's new "promised land."

In 1966, the Peruvian government signed a loan with the Inter-American Development Bank (IDB) to finance the colonization of the Tingo María–Tocache area, located in the departments of Huánuco and San Martín (see figure 7).[7] The project's goal was to develop some 85,000 new hectares of farmland and settle 5,250 families in the area. The total cost of developing the new colony and constructing much of the necessary infrastructure was set at U.S. $25 million. The IDB lent U.S. $15 million, and the Peruvian government contributed the balance. In 1969, the endeavor was expanded to cover Campanilla in San Martín department.

The ostensible goal of the colonization enterprise was laudable. Ultimately some 108,000 hectares (including Campanilla) were to be added to the nation's agricultural lands, all dedicated to the production of foodstuffs and, to a lesser extent, livestock. Thousands of unemployed or underemployed citizens were given an opportunity to forge a new future for themselves and their families. The state pledged to assist the colonists not only by providing basic infrastructure (primary and secondary roads), but also by building schools and health care centers. President Belaúnde further promised to furnish farming equipment and agricultural credit in the near future.

Unfortunately, Belaúnde's original plans for the colony were altered radically after he was ousted in an October 1968 coup by General Juan Velasco Alvarado. The new military administration brought tumultuous reforms to the country, including a new agrarian policy that prevented

FIGURE 7
The Upper Huallaga Valley:
Departments of San Martín and Huánuco

large-scale personal land ownership and emphasized collective and cooperative farming programs. These new policies and the institutions formed to implement them had a drastic impact on the Upper Huallaga colonization project. Although Belaúnde had planned for colonists' personal enterprise to give the project momentum, Velasco disregarded individual ownership in favor of collective efforts. Extensive territories were placed in the hands of cooperative partners, and credit was extended to the cooperative societies instead of private landholders. The direction of the project was also altered: livestock production, not agriculture, was made the primary emphasis of the new settlements.[8] All of these changes would create immense problems as time progressed.

Regional Development

Velasco's agrarian reform policies rendered the original plans for the Upper Huallaga obsolete and represented a severe setback for the region. Before making any topographical surveys of the land or cultural assessments of the new colonists, the military regime declared that the project was to be steered toward livestock production. To this end, 70 percent of the area in question was mandated for pasture land, up from the 39.8 percent originally envisioned by Belaúnde.[9] Under Velasco's scheme, large amounts of credit were allocated to the cooperatives for the purchase of cattle. The cooperative partners, mainly highland farmers and city migrants, were given no training or guidance for this enterprise, and, not surprisingly, they failed. When the cooperatives' debt burden became too heavy and the government failed to provide any educational support, cooperative members simply resigned and settled in the surrounding area as individual landowners. The peasants' mentality and work patterns were those adapted to life on the haciendas. Thus, they did not see it as their duty to shoulder the risks and burdens of the business. That was the responsibility of the cooperative, as it had been the responsibility of the land-owner or *hacendado* in their previous experience.[10]

Like the colonists who had taken up farming in the region during the Belaúnde administration, those who left the cooperatives to pursue agriculture in the area received absolutely no government support.

Even if Belaúnde's plan had been implemented following his ouster, there is still reason to suspect that the Huánuco-San Martín colonization project would have failed. Belaúnde, like many before him, saw the lushness of the rain-forest vegetation and surmised that the tropical soil below must be super-rich. He assumed that it would support agricultural production, which has not proven to be the case. Rain-forest soil is actually poor in nutrients and highly acidic; the dense vegetation is the result of highly complex interdependent systems that have evolved in the vegetation itself over thousands of years. Few substantial studies were available to point out this factor in the 1960s, however, when the project was begun, and none were commissioned to determine feasible crops that would preserve the scarce soil nutrients.[11]

The state also overlooked cultural factors pertinent to the migration of people into the Upper Huallaga region. It was assumed that the settlers were homogeneous in nature and would approach agriculture with the market-oriented mentality of other Western farmers. Again, the state's assumptions were tragically flawed. Migrants from the Andean highlands brought their own cultural framework to the region. They were oriented toward subsistence production and family rather than market-directed activities. Most migrants from urban areas had no agricultural experience whatsoever. Neither group was prepared for the inherent complexity of farming rain-forest soil.

The state's fundamental misunderstandings of tropical agriculture and cultural factors created extreme hardships for the new colonists and ultimately led to indiscriminate land use and serious destruction of forest resources.[12] Most of the colonists practiced some variation of the slash-and-burn method of cultivation. The nutrients created by burning the razed vegetation enriched the soil for up to three or four harvests, after which the exhausted soil could yield little more. At this point, most farmers moved to another plot and began the cycle anew; what was left of the original tract was usually destroyed by erosion shortly thereafter. Although this type of farming was sufficiently productive to support single families, it was nonetheless primitive and did not generate a surplus for market expansion as the government had expected. The state, on the other hand, was inefficient in arranging for training, technology, seed, and credit to be available to the colonists so that the desired surplus could be created. Individual farmers found it difficult to apply for loans on their own; the quality of their land was poor, and many had reneged on previous loans.

The few farmers who managed to generate a crop surplus for marketing purposes were exploited by marketing middlemen.[13] Generally, farmers sold their crops to these merchants before they were even planted, because they needed the money to buy seed and other supplies. Hence, the middlemen were able to set prices at will, often placing them below production cost. Other methods of marketing the crops were unavailable to the farmers, who had no means of transporting their harvests to market; the middlemen controlled that, too. The state, heavily involved in its multiple reform programs at the time, did not impose any sort of regulation, leaving the peasant farmers once again in a subordinate, exploited role.[14]

In short, the Upper Huallaga plan grossly underestimated the massive amounts of technical assistance and promotional credit that would be necessary for the project to flourish. Agricultural departments in the government did not provide any guidance about what plants were suitable for the valley's soil, and no educational programs were organized to teach the newcomers how to farm in the area. Roads built during the initial phases of the project were left unfinished and slowly decayed. The state failed in its principal mission of economically integrating the Upper Huallaga with the rest of Peru.

Emergence of the Coca Economy

The colonists discovered that there is one plant that will thrive in the Upper Huallaga Valley: coca. *Erythroxylum coca* has been cultivated by the Andean highland Indians for centuries. The leaves of the plant, when chewed, produce a slight feeling of euphoria. Under the Incas, coca leaves were believed to be endowed with magical powers and were used by the elite and the clergy for both religious and state ceremonies. Because of the mystical nature of the plant, however, the lower classes were not permitted to chew coca, except in cases of direct medicinal need or important religious ceremonies.

When the Catholic Church arrived in Peru with the Spanish conquistadors at the end of the fifteenth century, coca chewing was immediately discouraged because its religious use was considered blasphemous. This situation changed, though, when the Spanish learned that chewing coca leaves reduces sensitivity to hunger, cold, and fatigue. The conquistadors immediately reversed the Church's stance against coca and began providing it in large quantities to the enslaved Indians working in their gold and silver mines. From this time on, coca chewing spread widely throughout the Andean population. The phenomenon was enhanced by the capacity of the leaf to suppress hunger after the Spanish had disrupted the country's normal foodstuff production by forcing most of the Indian peasants into the mines.

Today the inhabitants of highland rural Peru continue the widespread practice of masticating coca. As before, it helps lessen the drudgery of labor and hunger. The present work day, from 7 A.M. to 5 P.M., includes several breaks exclusively for coca chewing. At one time, salaries were even paid in kilograms of coca leaves. A 1970 survey showed that 15 percent of the population of Peru chews coca leaves daily.[15] Although the government has mandated that coca chewing should be slowly but firmly eliminated, little or nothing has been done toward achieving this goal. To implement a policy of this type would be something akin to outlawing coffee consumption in the United States.

When Indian peasants migrated to the Upper Huallaga from the Andean highlands, they brought with them the ancestral practices of their culture, including coca cultivation. Thus, the coca plant was first introduced to the upper rain forest as part of the colonists' subsistence agriculture; it was grown solely for personal consumption and light trade. Over the years, coca production grew, and by the 1970s the Upper Huallaga had become recognized as the principal region of coca cultivation in the country. The plant is grown legally for Empresa Nacional de la Coca (ENACO), Peru's government-controlled coca company, which markets the leaves and their by-products for medicinal purposes and widely consumed coca tea. Coca is also grown illegally for sale to drug traffickers who refine it into cocaine. Both practices, predominantly the latter, helped strengthen the regional economy while fostering increased local coca consumption. Peasants growing coffee and cacao soon began to produce coca as well, because it allowed them to subsidize their otherwise meager incomes.

The Coca Plant

In spite of poor soil conditions, the coca plant thrives in the valley area. This geographical region is one of the few in the world that provides the particular conditions necessary for *Erythroxylum coca* to flourish: high humidity, a constant temperature around 65°F., and an unusual variety of soil that is unsuitable for almost all other cash crops. The coca bush, when mature (usually around 18 months after planting), reaches a height of approximately 12 feet, but is often trimmed to six or nine feet to simplify the harvesting of its leaves. Otherwise, it requires virtually no care at all. This unusually durable plant will yield three to four harvests a year during its life span, which may last up to 30 years.[16] As illegal cocaine use increased in the United States, coca production became increasingly profitable to the otherwise struggling colonists. Hungry for the leaves that yield cocaine paste, traffickers would pay growers up to 10 times the price received for other crops – often in advance. By the late 1970s, when international demand for cocaine began to soar, a growing number of colonists turned to coca cultivation to ease their economic problems.

Expansion of Coca Cultivation

In 1978, under pressure from the United States, the military government of President Francisco Morales Bermudez (1975–1980) became concerned about the quantities of coca being produced illegally and enacted legislation to eliminate illicit coca cultivation – Decree Law 22095.[17] Under the name "Green Sea" (*Verde Mar*), a large-scale operation was mounted to destroy all the large coca farms. In reality, all that was accomplished was the eradication of 60 of the estimated 12,000 hectares of Upper Huallaga coca fields then in existence.[18] Spurred by the ever-increasing area under coca cultivation, the Peruvian government declared the departments of Huánuco, San Martín, and parts of Loreto under a state of emergency in 1980.[19] Government forces were ordered to confiscate land, destroy coca crops, and incarcerate resisting farmers and landowners.[20] These measures proved almost entirely counterproductive. Besides being logistically impossible to fulfill, the mandate of the police had the unexpected countereffect of causing higher prices for black market coca leaves. The increased profits, in turn, converted even more peasants into coca planters. These individuals accepted the slight inherent risks as a small price to pay for the additional income.

Interestingly enough, the massive expansion of coca cultivation has altered neither the structural characteristics of the peasant-based economy nor the farmers' growing techniques. Although coca sales have greatly boosted settlers' incomes, most growers have not expanded their fields and continue to rely upon unpaid family members for labor. Moreover, few have adopted modernized farming techniques. The typical coca grower continues to be a colonist of Andean origin whose production is destined primarily for local sale or personal consumption.[21]

By 1988, coca cultivation was estimated to incorporate 211,000 hectares in the Upper Huallaga Valley alone – an enormous increase from the 1980 total of roughly 28,000.[22] Not surprisingly, this growth has led the valley to become a major center of cocaine-paste production. The two changes combined have brought government presence in the valley to an all-time high. The farmers and colonists, already at odds with the government, have now become further agitated as special police units are ordered to destroy their most profitable source of income, while offering them no credit or technical assistance in developing a replacement crop.[23]

Sendero Luminoso Recruits Popular Support

Sendero's presence in the Upper Huallaga dates from the early 1980s. Following the movement's general modus operandi, Sendero militants moved into the area and settled quietly among the populace. Once established, they began to share the problems faced by the settlers, fostering trust in the insurgency among them. Simultaneously, these Senderistas began to undermine the government by criticizing its errors and inconsistencies. DIRCOTE sources believe that it was Osmán Morote Barrionuevo who took steps to establish the region as Sendero's northeastern front in 1983–1984. By 1985, Sendero had become an armed presence in the region. The movement's strength and support has continued to increase since that time, filling the political vacuum long present in the Upper Huallaga region. Predictably, Sendero's visibility led to heightened military presence in the area – a development that Sendero Luminoso has also exploited to its own advantage.

The Peruvian government unwittingly fueled the growers' resentment by implementing a number of programs designed to reduce or eradicate coca grown in the Upper Huallaga. In 1980, two years after the law prohibiting the free
cultivation of coca was passed, the state also instituted the
Special Project for the Upper Huallaga (Proyecto Especial
Alto Huallaga or PEAH). The purpose of the project was to
reintroduce other cash crops into the region in hopes that
the impact of coca reduction might be assuaged. PEAH
has failed so far. Another program, the Agreement for
the Control and Reduction of Coca in the Upper Huallaga
or CORAH, was introduced under U.S. auspices in 1981.
CORAH's goal was the total eradication of coca in the valley region. Although the program itself enjoyed only limited
success, it has further agitated the local population. A highly mobile narcotics police unit was introduced simultaneously. Known as the Mobile Rural Patrol Unit (Unidad Mo-
vil de Patrullaje Rural or UMOPAR), this new division of the
Civil Guard was immediately perceived as a threat by local
people and added considerably to their hostility toward the
state. In the eyes of the farmers, these regulations and programs are aimed at taking away their only means of survival—coca cultivation. The presence of the state, conspicuous-
ly absent when needed, has thus become an element of
alienation among the inhabitants of the Upper Huallaga.

The group that actually benefited from the state's antinarcotics initiatives was Sendero Luminoso. The government programs provided the insurgency with a fortuitous
opportunity to denounce the United States as the primary
culprit for the growers' problems. The rebels emphasize to
the Huallaga populace that cocaine consumption is not a
problem in Peru, only in the decadent United States. U.S.
Drug Enforcement Agency (DEA) agents in the region
have encountered understandable animosity. "You'll have
imperialists cutting down coca trees in front of a crying
peasant woman," said one experienced agent in a *New York
Times* interview. "Mao could not have thought of anything
better."[24]

Sendero also contends that it protects the growers from

exploitation by the cocaine syndicate. Working in collusion with the Colombian cocaine mafias, local producers and traffickers have disarmed many of the local police and local authorities with bribes or coercion. They have also developed paramilitary forces equipped with the most modern weapons and communications systems available, allowing them to act freely with minimal risk. It is, therefore, the peasants who bear the risk of being arrested and incarcerated, or, worse, having their crops destroyed by the police.[25] The traffickers are adamant that the growers are paid well to cultivate the leaves and to avoid interference from UMOPAR and other police detachments. Therefore, those who are unable to deliver their crops as promised are routinely executed, their bodies thrown into a river or left in a field.[26] These deaths are meant to serve both as reprisals and warnings. Before Sendero's arrival, the growers had practically no recourse against these abuses. The rebels provided support for farmers seeking to organize themselves against both the police and the traffickers. Organization has also made it possible for the growers to negotiate better prices for their coca leaves.[27] Finally, Sendero's armed struggle aids the colonists psychologically, giving them an outlet for their violent animosity toward the government forces.

For these reasons, violence is rife in the Upper Huallaga. The majority of the growers are armed, some with automatic weapons, to defend themselves against the variety of threats they must continually confront.[28] For those unable to defend themselves, Sendero once again is available to provide assistance.

Growers, Traffickers, and Terrorists

Each hectare of coca planted in the Upper Huallaga produces at least two metric tons of leaves annually. Growers sell each ton of leaves to middlemen for around U.S. $600.[29] These intermediaries then transport the leaves to crude clandestine laboratories for processing into cocaine paste. The *cocales*, or coca farms, of the valley encompass some 211,000 hectares of coca fields; of these, approximately 200,000 generate coca that enters the illicit drug trade.[30]

A study of the cocaine industry released by the Peruvian government in 1986 calculates that each metric ton of dried coca leaves yields 21 kilograms of semirefined cocaine paste.[31] The paste is purchased by traffickers, who are usually associated with international smuggling rings, for U.S. $890 per kilogram.[32] These traffickers transport the paste to hidden laboratories in the rain forests of Peru, Ecuador, Colombia, and, increasingly, Brazil, where it is refined into pure cocaine hydrochloride. Approximately three kilograms of paste are required to produce one kilogram of pure cocaine. One metric ton of coca leaves is required to produce seven kilograms of cocaine. The finished product is then smuggled by a myriad of methods into the United States, where it is sold to wholesalers in Miami for at least U.S. $10,000 per kilogram.[33]

These figures for coca leaves and cocaine paste yield an estimated value of U.S. $28 billion for Peruvian cocaine upon reaching the United States. According to this projection, cocaine produced in Peru would yield gross revenues of approximately U.S. $7.48 billion for the paste producers and local traffickers. After paying growers U.S. $240 million for cultivating the coca, revenues would amount to roughly U.S. $7.24 billion (see figure 8). Of course, there are a great many other costs—chemicals (to process the leaves into paste), protection, bribes, transportation, and the smuggling of the cocaine paste past authorities. Nevertheless, the gross amount of hard currency entering Peru through these illegitimate channels is equal to approximately 20 percent of the legitimate Peruvian GNP.[34] Foreign exchange earnings from copper, Peru's largest legal export, pale by comparison; they amount to only 1.4 percent of the GNP.[35] The immense potential for profits has led coca cultivation to expand over almost the entire valley, affecting the departments of San Martín, Huánuco, Ucayali, and Loreto.

FIGURE 8
Profits from the Production and Sale of
Peruvian Cocaine, 1988
(in U.S. dollars)

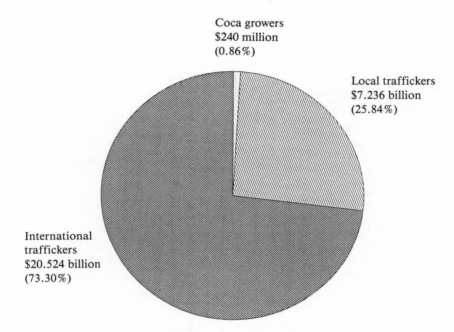

Coca growers
$240 million
(0.86%)

Local traffickers
$7.236 billion
(25.84%)

International
traffickers
$20.524 billion
(73.30%)

Source: Author's calculations based on data from sources in notes 29 to 33 of chapter 6.

As of 1989, the Upper Huallaga ranks as the primary region of coca cultivation in the world.

The massive influx of so-called narcodollars, often referred to as the "coca economy," has given the local traffickers unprecedented power and created abnormal economic activity in the region.[36] Armed with a seemingly endless supply of dollars, the traffickers can move about as they please, paying off anyone who attempts to interfere with their activities. Equally damaging is the distortion of consumption patterns that has emerged in the region, causing prices to become grossly inflated and local markets to become disrupted. Although the markets of most rural Peruvian towns are lined with vendors of foodstuffs and clothing, those of Tingo María, Tocache, and other valley towns sell Japanese radios, cassette players, and other electronic goods – all at ever-escalating prices. The salaries of domestic help in these regional towns are greater than those of teachers in Lima. Houses that appear to be slums from the outside may be furnished with modern stereo equipment or wide-screen televisions.

According to an oft-told story, the owner of a Japanese appliances franchise in the town of Uchiza won the company's annual regional sales competition. When the Japanese representatives arrived in Uchiza to present him with the award, they were shocked to find that the store owner used no advertising and that his store was located in the poorest section of town. Asked the secret to his amazing sales record, he replied, "I open the store and people come. They pay the exact amount owed in cash. People here have a lot of money."[37] Similarly, the smallest of towns in the coca region may boast several branch outlets of Lima's major banks – all strategically placed to capitalize on the high volume of dollar transactions.

The estimated remaining U.S. $20.52 billion generated by the sale of Peruvian-originated cocaine remains in the hands of international traffickers and dealers in the United States. Most of this money enters the international economy after being laundered. Although this sum is equal to roughly 57 percent of the Peruvian GNP, little if any of it is repatriated.

Benefits for Coca Growers

Coca farmers initially associate with Sendero Luminoso for one fundamental reason: it is in their economic interest to do so. Ministry of the Interior data indicates that there are close to 66,000 families cultivating coca in the Upper Huallaga.[38] Given only two full harvests per year (a low yield), the average annual family earnings come to about U.S. $3,636 before expenses, a handsome sum compared to Peru's per capita income of U.S. $1,000. This amount is substantially more than could be earned with any of the usual legal crops, such as coffee, tea, cacao, or citrus.[39] Because some families own up to 25 hectares, coca production may, in fact, prove quite lucrative.[40] Colonists are unwilling to give up such an earning opportunity and are understandably antagonistic toward government attempts to curb or alleviate coca production.

Sendero Luminoso is a welcome solution to the farmers' problems because it offers protection. Although the group's ideological commitment to helping the rootless and exploited may appeal to the colonists, the growers' allegiance to the movement appears to be anchored more in economics than in ideology. The insurgency has shrewdly won the farmers' confidence by easing their two primary burdens: the coca-eradication programs initiated by the government and the exploitation from traffickers and their intermediaries.

Eradication initiatives have posed great danger for the coca farmers. Besides the economic hardships that are caused when the police actually destroy crops, growers also face almost certain death from the traffickers if they are unable to deliver as promised. Because this type of extortion was the farmers' most pressing concern, Sendero has devoted much effort to alleviating the problem. The insurgency has also employed its well-practiced terrorist tactics to deal with UMOPAR, the regional police, and CORAH, the primary eradication program. The methods implemented to achieve this end are very similar to those used in Ayacucho in prior years. The Senderistas, aided by locals, have assassinated officials and dynamited police and army garrisons.[41] Because the government forces are often undermanned (the Upper Huallaga is a large area that is very difficult to patrol completely), terrorist techniques have been successful. Outgunned, the police may have no option but to momentarily vacate, leaving Sendero Luminoso in

political control of an area and the farmers free from government interference. In most instances, the power of the state
is eventually reasserted.

Employing a combination of terrorist tactics and organizational skill, Sendero has also assisted the growers in
confronting their other primary dilemma: exploitation from
the traffickers. This conflict arose as a result of the traffickers' heavy use of coercive violence and complete unwillingness to negotiate prices. Besides the informal "death sentence" imposed when a grower proved unable to deliver, the
traffickers employed well-armed gangs in every coca region
to discourage farmers from organizing themselves. When
farmers did, on occasion, try to organize, the gangs would
move in, forcefully break them up, and kill the leaders.
Gang members were also accused of extorting farmers and
their families, threatening them with violence if they refused to comply. Sendero Luminoso, militarily stout and
well-versed in strong-arm tactics, has been able to resolve
both of these problems. Generally, its approach is to move
into a town with at least 30 armed men, band the population together for rhetorical harangues, question the townspeople about both local authorities and gang members, and
then banish or execute these unfortunate individuals. General assemblies (*comités populares*) composed of Sendero
loyalists are then placed in command of the settlements.

Once the movement has secured a sufficient number of
towns in a region, the zone is "liberated."[42] Liberation entails
expelling all police and military detachments and dispers-
ing any remaining traffickers' gangs. Normally Sendero will
first ask the traffickers to disband the gangs; if they resist,
the guerrillas will simply kill gang members one at a time
until those remaining have no alternative but to flee or join
Sendero. Many opt for the latter choice. Once the region is
fully under their control, the Senderistas are able to organize the growers and negotiate higher coca prices with the
cocaine-paste producers. Interestingly enough, when this
stage is reached, the traffickers also see it in their best
interest to work with Sendero.

Benefits for Traffickers

Much skepticism has been expressed regarding Sendero's alliance with the drug traffickers. It seems paradoxical that a self-righteous and, in a sense, puritanical group like Sendero Luminoso would associate with the capitalist-oriented traffickers. The insurgency's rhetorical search for higher ideals and consistent denunciation of drug consumption appear utterly irreconcilable with the narcotics trade. Nevertheless, it is apparent that a mutually beneficial alliance does indeed exist. Sendero, observing that the vast majority of the cocaine produced in the valley is destined for the United States, justifies its participation in the drug trade by explaining that narcotics contribute to the corrosion and demoralization of the "Yankee imperialists."[43]

Sendero offers cocaine producers and traffickers three important benefits: discipline among the growers, protection from police and military interference, and the promise of further government destabilization. Because of the heavy influx of dollars, the regions where coca is grown are characterized by violence, widespread alcohol consumption, and general disorderly conduct. The traffickers' gangs had been able to ensure that coca quotas would be met in spite of this chaotic life-style, but Sendero has actually increased coca production by enforcing a more rigorous work ethic. Upon securing an area, the rebels, adhering to their severe rhetoric, immediately close the local bars, discos, and brothels, execute homosexuals, and banish prostitutes. Time previously spent in hedonistic pursuits is redirected toward work on the farms. The traffickers are thus assured of a more reliable source of the raw materials essential to their trade.

Sendero's efforts to agitate and destabilize the government force the state to devote more attention, more military force, and more money to fighting the insurgency. Because Sendero poses a far greater threat to Peru's national security than the traffickers do, those involved in advanced stages of drug production know that the insurgency provides them with a margin of freedom. They have realized that it is beneficial to ally themselves with Sendero Luminoso, and they have done so throughout the Upper Huallaga. Unhindered by government interference, both growers and traffickers are able to work and transact more efficiently in regions under the insurgency's control.

The traffickers have also utilized the guerrillas to protect their many clandestine airstrips scattered throughout the region. Small planes use these hidden airports to transport the cocaine paste from Peru to processing centers in Colombia and Ecuador, where it is processed into pure cocaine hydrochloride ready for export to the United States. An average planeload may carry as much as 500 kilograms of the cocaine paste.[44] Planes are also used to import chemicals needed to produce the cocaine paste. Many of these chemicals, which may be difficult to purchase from the United States, are now acquired from Brazil. An official from the Ministry of the Interior has set the number of hidden runways at 168, though there are certainly more.[45] Compounding the problem is the fact that small aircraft traffic in the region is completely unregulated (the police have neither radar nor armed aircraft), and planes come and go completely at will. On the occasions when a police plane does sight a presumed trafficker aircraft and orders it to land, its radio commands are often answered only by derisive laughter.[46] Logically, Sendero receives a percentage for its part in protecting narcotics production and transport.

Benefits for Sendero

Sendero, on the other hand, also benefits greatly from its association with the traffickers — arguably more than any of the other parties involved. Besides its commitment to undermining the United States through drugs, Sendero's presence in the valley has facilitated recruitment of hundreds of new supporters and access to previously unavailable funds.

The regional colonists seem to have accepted the movement's overtures. As the living conditions in towns improve in the wake of Sendero's intervention, growers in surrounding municipalities have become more open to the insurgency's presence. Ironically, for many of these people Sendero Luminoso is the only political entity capable of keeping the regional economy active, free from government eradication programs and gang harassment.[47] This fact, coupled with the long-standing frustration of the Peruvian rural underclass toward the government, has sealed Sendero's success in the region. The growers now look to Sendero almost exclusively when new conflicts arise. The Upper Huallaga may be counted as one of Sendero's greatest successes; it can be considered among the movement's strongest support bases.

Sendero Luminoso, however, has done more than simply take possession of the territory. It has also won the hearts and minds of the inhabitants, adding hundreds of names to the movement's roster of sympathizers and militants. Many of these people have now become interested in the movement for ideological as well as economic reasons. Although people in the Upper Huallaga once assumed social status by imitating the traffickers (wearing flowered shirts, white pants, and dark glasses), this image has changed. Status may now be acquired by speaking religiously about revolution, even though an understanding of the concept may be minimal.[48] The Senderistas in the Upper Huallaga are content with this situation. "The important thing," explained a militant, "is not that [the people] understand why they are fighting, but rather that they are willing and ready to fight." The objective, from Sendero's point of view, is to agitate the region's masses. "Once they have been stirred up," continues the same Senderista, "they will become blind and do whatever the party commands."[49] The popular guerrilla army in the Huallaga has been organized into four battalions (*columnas*) and is now thought to number more than a thousand. Security sources mention that militants and commanders (*mandos*) have been brought in from other regions of the country — Ayacucho, Pasco, Junín, and Lima — to train and organize the growing number of new followers.[50]

The alliance with the traffickers also works to Sendero's economic advantage. It is well known that the insurgency charges the traffickers for regulating and protecting coca production. Recently, it has also become apparent that the rebels have expanded their operations, providing armed protection to cocaine-paste producers and those trafficking in the final cocaine product. The actual figures that the guerrillas are paid for their services are obviously difficult to determine, but are generally thought to range in the tens of millions of dollars.[51]

In some areas Sendero has also branched into other phases of the cocaine-paste production and distribution process. In Xión, for example, the rebels have become involved in currency exchange.[52] Most deals transacted in this area are arranged and carried out by associates of the Colombian cartels. These intermediaries come to Peru with U.S. dollars, which must then be changed to Peruvian *intis*. Originally, all currency exchange was completed by offices of national banks located in Xión. After Sendero began to govern the area, however, this practice was forbidden. The movement designated certain individuals with whom currencies could be exchanged; no others were permitted. Again, Sendero receives a certain percentage of the exchanges for providing a steady flow of business. Bankers were livid upon learning of the arrangement, but there was literally no recourse they could take without endangering personnel and other branch offices. Significantly, Sendero's access to and control of hard currency (U.S. dollar) transactions comes at a time when the government's hard currency reserves are gravely depleted.[53]

Exactly what the movement does with the vast sums earned from these endeavors is unknown, although it is logical to assume that much of the income goes toward the purchase of arms and supplies. The Sendero militants of the Upper Huallaga form what is probably the best-armed militia in all of Peru. By comparison the government police and military officers who have been sent to the Upper Huallaga to combat the insurgency are underpaid and undersupported. Because Sendero Luminoso is in better shape financially than the government, and because Sendero is able to extract support from the local populace by means inaccessible to the government, the police and the military forces are poorly prepared to counter Sendero. Sendero militants are supported well materially and psychologically; the forces of law and order are not.[54]

Sendero has destabilized the government, taken additional national territory under its control, and added many new adherents to its ranks. It has befriended a people whose government had all but abandoned them; it has helped reactivate a stumbling sector of the economy, albeit illegally; and it has succeeded in undermining state control in a relatively young and important region of the country. The Upper Huallaga, in effect, has virtually become a state-within-a-state, governed by Sendero and supported economically by the cocaine producers. For the drug traffickers, the valley has become a secure place to perpetuate their trade. For Sendero Luminoso, it has become a stronghold of the revolution.

The Power of Narcoterrorism

The two groups working together—Sendero Luminoso and the cocaine syndicate—have given rise to a powerful new phenomenon in Peru: narcoterrorism. This alliance is consummately logical to both entities, because they share certain goals—destabilization of the government, discipline among the growers, and liberation from the meddling of police and the military. The informal governing system set up by the two groups in the Upper Huallaga has actually proven quite successful. In effect, a quasi-state functioning within the Peruvian state has emerged in the region, lending legitimacy in the eyes of the populace to two marginal social groups that, in reality, are delinquents.

Ironically, almost every attempt made by the government to undermine the narcoterrorist alliance has been ineffectual and has played directly into the hands of the narcoterrorists. When the government tries to eradicate coca, additional hectares are planted to prevent a shortage; when the military moves in to secure towns, excesses committed by soldiers alienate the townspeople; when the government tries to obstruct the cocaine trade, the growers become hostile as their source of income is jeopardized. In all of these cases, the people of the Upper Huallaga have increasingly begun to look to Sendero Luminoso as a protector and friend.

Sendero's Rapid Rise to Power

Sendero's link to drug interests in the valley first surfaced in December 1983 when three members of the Peruvian Civil Guard (Guardia Civil del Perú) were murdered in the attack on the Civil Guard station in Nuevo Progreso.[55] At first, the authorities disregarded the incident as just another case of random violence on the part of narcotics traffickers operating in the area. Even later, when evidence surfaced indicating that the officers had been killed by insurgents protecting drug activity, the case was written off as an isolated incident. By 1987, however, the power and breadth of the narcoterrorist alliance had become undeniable. Whole regions of the valley had been wrested from government authority as the insurgency secured town after town, replacing local officials with it own supporters and imposing its own peculiar category of "justice." Working in collusion with drug interests, entire provinces of the region had become "liberated zones."[56]

The growth of narcoterrorism has paralleled the explosive expansion of coca cultivation in the Huallaga. Initially, coca farms were found primarily in the upper sector of the valley, dotting the area between Tingo María and Campanilla (including Tocache and Uchiza). By late 1988, the production of coca had spread to the Central Huallaga (Juanjuí, Bellavista, and Picote) as well as the neighboring Lower Mayo Valley (Tarapoto, Tabaloso, Sisa, and Lamas).[57] Throughout this area, the violence that accompanies contraband and large sums of money caused uneasiness, insecurity, and hostility among the people and has disrupted their behavior patterns. Those involved in the coca cultivation were intimidated by the traffickers' gangs and avaricious cocaine-paste producers. Neither the police nor the military could ameliorate these problems, but Sendero did. Entire battalions of armed Senderistas entered troubled towns and literally took them over. Those residing in the towns generally welcomed the intervention, realizing that the Senderistas would impose order and free them to continue growing coca without further obstacles. "From [the day Sendero Luminoso came]," commented a coca-plantation employee to a Lima journalist, "our salaries went up and there aren't so many abuses. The Senderistas come every week and ask the townspeople how they are being treated by the growers, if there have been abuses, what problems we have."[58]

A Region Transformed

Many of the towns that Sendero has annexed are located along Belaúnde's famous "Marginal Highway." Two of particular significance are Tocache and Uchiza; both serve as major transaction centers for cocaine paste and both were dramatically taken over by the insurgency in mid-1987. In these towns, as in others that the insurgency has seized, the new allegiance of the population was immediately evidenced by the widespread appearance of Sendero graffiti. The walls of the towns are blanketed with revolutionary slogans: *Coca or death, Glory to the heroes of the revolution, Viva el Presidente Gonzalo, Out with the Yankees, Viva la Revolución*, and, of course, the ubiquitous hammer and sickle.[59] Vehicles are also subject to the rain of graffiti. To drive a car or truck unadorned by the hammer-and-sickle emblem is tantamount to declaring oneself an enemy of the revolution. Efforts to paint over the rebel propaganda have proven fruitless. Twenty-four hours after a massive cleanup campaign was completed in Tocache (all buildings and public monuments were restored), the graffiti were replaced. This time, however, Sendero let it be known that anyone who attempted to remove or paint over the slogans would be executed.

Many stretches of the Marginal Highway itself have also been claimed by Sendero Luminoso. Numerous bridges have been dynamited to prevent "feudalists" from delivering goods produced through "exploitation of the masses" to Lima and to block military detachments attempting to reach the Huallaga Valley. The ruins of these bridges uniformly bear the inscription *Viva el Presidente Gonzalo*. On other sections of the highway, ditches have been dug into the road at 100 meter intervals. Alongside these ditches are improvised defenses that allow hidden Sendero militants to ambush unrecognized vehicles as they slow down. And, along every portion of the highway, one may find painted revolutionary slogans and the hammer-and-sickle insignia, often carved into the pavement itself.

The insurgency exhaustively inspects almost all vehicles traveling on the road within what has become its territory. Rebels scrutinize cars and trucks with a thoroughness not unlike that encountered at an international boundary-line checkpoint. Vehicles are stopped and passengers are required to present identification. These are checked meticulously. If a person is identified as a member of the police or armed forces (or any other enemy of the insurgency for that matter), he is executed on the spot. Vehicles not bearing the hammer-and-sickle insignia may be subject to attack and burning; at times the roadsides have been littered with the burnt-out shells of cars and trucks. If, however, all is found to be in order when a party is held up, the travelers are allowed to continue after listening to an ideological lecture. Given that the Marginal Highway is the primary road connecting all the towns in the Huallaga Valley, then joining with roads to the coast (to Lima and other coastal commercial centers), the significance of Sendero's control over it must not be underestimated.

The authority that the insurgency has assumed over

the coca-producing region has made the area safe for all facets of trafficking activity. In fact, the traffickers, convinced that Sendero may offer at least a temporary solution to some of their problems, have even assisted the movement in defeating the other primary revolutionary group in the area: the Tupac Amaru Revolutionary Movement (Movimiento Revolucionario Tupac Amaru or MRTA).[60] Since the early 1980s, the MRTA had competed with Sendero Luminoso for control of certain areas of the valley and the political support of the peasant population within them. The traffickers recognized that Sendero, as the more powerful of the two groups, was more likely to protect their interests in the valley for a sustained period. Therefore, by launching a series of joint attacks, Sendero and the drug interests were able to force the MRTA out of the primary coca-growing areas farther north toward Juanjuí in the department of San Martín.[61] Although this turf battle appears to fluctuate back and forth between the two, there is little doubt that Sendero — backed by the traffickers — continues to maintain the upper hand.

By January 1989, Sendero Luminoso's sphere of influence had spread east to the river-port town of Pucallpa, thus crowning the insurgency's control of almost the entire Huallaga Valley.[62] From Tarapoto in the north to Tingo María in the south, drug interests, protected by the guerrillas, now operate with almost complete freedom in the upper rain-forest departments of San Martín, Huánuco, and Ucayali. Narcoterrorism, the dangerous alliance between the well-organized Sendero insurgents and the well-financed drug syndicate, allows both groups to support one another while furthering their respective objectives. In the process, the stability and legitimacy of the Peruvian government is greatly undermined. The effects of this association are already transforming the Huallaga population's perception of the elected government. Because no realistic, long-term strategy for fighting narcoterrorism has been formulated, the threat stands only to grow in the coming years.[63]

Government Response in the Huallaga Valley

Tackling the Huallaga narcoterrorism dilemma is, by nature, a daunting task. The Peruvian government, beset by a
massive economic crisis and the threat of the Sendero
Luminoso insurgency throughout the rest of the country,
has understandably experienced difficulty in devising an
effective counteroffensive policy. The situation is further
aggravated by the state's refusal to acknowledge and address narcoterrorism as a single social, military, and political entity. Although the emergence of narcoterrorism has
been generally recognized since 1984, the state's actions are
inconsistent with this recognition. Instead of formulating a
policy to combat narcoterrorism as a whole, the government insists upon addressing narcotics and terrorism as
separate elements. Drug trafficking in Peru is fought by the
police forces. Terrorism is considered a threat to national
security and is therefore fought by the military. In practice,
the police and the military utterly refuse to cooperate with
each other. On occasion, they have even been known to obstruct one another at critical junctures of an operation,
further fueling the rivalry that exists between them. As a
result, the narcoterrorist alliance currently faces little tan-
gible challenge from the Peruvian government.

The first operation to counter narcoterrorism began
quite by accident when the Peruvian government launched
an antinarcotics operation in May 1984 in the Upper Huallaga. With substantial funding from the DEA, "Operation
Bronco" was initially envisioned by the state as a 15-day
siege in which the police were to attack all levels of the
valley's narcotics industry. Although Bronco did not result
in substantial drug seizures, the operation destroyed 25
clandestine airstrips and sacked several hidden laborato-
ries. As the attack was carried out, the connection between
Sendero Luminoso and the cocaine industry was revealed to
be much more profound than previously thought. An
alarmed Ministry of the Interior extended Operation Bron-

co's activities to 30 days and expanded its mandate to encompass narcoterrorism. But, as a police officer said, "How can we know who is who?"[64]

Concerned that the U.S. government would not approve of its predesignated financial aid being used to combat the insurgency as well as the narcotics industry, the minister of the interior limited the duties of the police in the Upper Huallaga to antinarcotics activities.[65] At the same time (1984), however, the army was called into the area to fight the insurgency. The latter move ultimately proved disastrous, as bribes from the drug syndicate gradually assured that army personnel would protect rather than combat them. It was later revealed that the army general in charge of the operation and 13 of his aides were actually colluding with the drug traffickers.[66] This type of jurisdictional conflict, augmented by the extant and intense interservice rivalries, continues to hinder initiatives against narcoterrorism.

Following Operation Bronco, Sendero-related violence grew incrementally throughout the Upper Huallaga. The Peruvian media reported that much of the turmoil was linked to the drug trade. The media's assumptions were widely accepted, despite gaps in the evidence necessary to prove the connection conclusively. Three years later, by mid-1987, the situation had become critical; persistent attacks on police stations and the taking over of towns forced the Peruvian government to intervene again.

State of Emergency

The next major antinarcoterrorism initiative was launched in July 1987 in response to steadily increasing violence in the region. Although the government had long been aware that decisive steps were necessary, it took a major surprise attack by Sendero to spur the state into action. On May 31, 1987, 200 armed Sendero guerrillas stormed the Civil Guard station in Uchiza. Six police officers and four civilians were killed, and the entire station was destroyed by dynamite. This act confirmed what many state officials had long feared: the state was no longer the dominant power in the Upper Huallaga. As a result, an immediate state of emergency — coded "Operation Lightning" (*Relámpago*) — was declared over the Tocache-Uchiza area in the department of San Martín.[67] Although it was a Sendero initiative that actually prompted the implementation of Operation Lightning, it was the police, not the military, who were put in charge of the operation. Additional units of the Civil Guard and PIP were sent from Lima to bolster the forces already present, but the military was left out entirely. In effect, the government was attributing the source of the problem to the narcotics trade (Tocache and Uchiza are both major centers of drug transactions), not to the insurgency.

For a short time, the police were able to establish order in the emergency region. The traffickers moved to other areas to buy coca and produce cocaine paste, and the Senderistas, relatively popular among the inhabitants of the area, simply faded into the natural cover. Over the next few months, the sales of coca leaves and cocaine paste slowed significantly in Tocache-Uchiza, a change that soon led to a new problem. When the growers realized that the state of emergency would hinder their economic productivity, they grew hostile toward the police and, with the help of Sendero, began to work against them. The police soon found themselves outgunned and outmanned by the insurgency, even though it was the traffickers that they had come to apprehend. This situation, coupled with a burst of MRTA activity in the area, added an explosive new dimension to the regional conflict.[68]

The García administration, alarmed by the apparent total disorder in the Upper Huallaga, reacted by declaring the entire department of San Martín under a state of emergency in early November 1987. This time, however, the operation was placed into the hands of the military, not the police. This policy change meant that the emphasis of the fight had been shifted from the narcotics traffickers to Sendero Luminoso and MRTA. Once more, the government refused to recognize and act against the narcoterrorist alliance. Because of interagency squabbling, no region in the emergency zone is under the jurisdiction of both the army and the police; therefore, at least one of narcoterrorism's two hands is free to maneuver in any given area.

When the state of emergency was declared, turf battles within the state forces escalated sharply. The knottiness of the situation stems from the fact that Tocache and Uchiza are both located within the department of San Martín, which was entirely assigned to the Fifth Regional Army Command. Under the state of emergency, the Ministry of the Interior was hesitant to place army officers in command of an area (Tocache-Uchiza) that had been under emergency police jurisdiction for four months. Fearing such a move might negate earlier progress against drug interests in the area, the ministry left Tocache-Uchiza under police control, but redesignated the area a military subzone of the Second Regional Army Command based in Huánuco. Thus, in the subzone, antinarcotics operations continue to be executed by the police, while the army simultaneously battles Sendero in the department completely surrounding it. Here, the complexities of fighting narcoterrorism are manifest, as are the deleterious effects of such profound interservice rivalries.[69]

Two years after the state of emergency was first declared in the area, Sendero Luminoso continues to grow in strength, and the narcoterrorism phenomenon continues to spread. Sendero's strategy is rooted in the invisibility principle: the Senderistas wear no uniforms to distinguish them from inhabitants of the area; they have no base camps that would give the army opportunity for debilitating counterattacks; and they shy away from face-to-face fighting, preferring surprise attacks and bombings. Government officials have now realized that the fight against narcoterrorism is being lost, largely because there is no comprehensive program to counter it.[70] State offensive measures are further impaired by the quantities of narcodollars in the region, which are used to corrupt all levels of police and military personnel. The traffickers have used the corrosive influence of their wealth to turn the armed forces against one another even more, a shrewd maneuver that has even led to confrontations between UMOPAR and army officers.[71]

Military intervention in the Upper Huallaga has also further alienated the populace from the state. The people of the region, already hostile toward government eradication programs and police occupation, are understandably aggravated by the ominous shadow of the military. The army has become notorious for roughly handling the populace it is supposedly defending. Sendero Luminoso, in contrast, is well positioned to manipulate the peoples' distrust of the state.

Many of the army's excesses, for which it became infamous in Ayacucho, have been repeated in the Upper Huallaga. Fear of the government forces has led people to view the army as the enemy. Peasants and townspeople will regularly flee their houses and hide in the woods when a military patrol approaches, waiting until the soldiers have left before returning. The district attorneys' offices in the provinces of the Huallaga area receive daily complaints of army abuses, with "disappearances" among the most frequently reported.

Overlapping Jurisdictions

The state of emergency, as it currently functions, tragically subordinates the legal apparatus in the emergency zones to the Political and Military Command. Because the respective powers of the Public Ministry and the Political and Military Command remain confused in these zones, there is a lack of cooperation within the forces of law and order.[72]

If the rights of citizens living under the state of emergency are violated by the state's military arm and these citizens appeal to the state's judicial arm for protection, then they are soon disappointed. District attorneys and their assistants are categorically denied access to areas the military has defined as "critical," such as the army barracks and jails housing the accused. Soldiers are under orders not to assist investigators, and cooperation from police forces operating in the area is virtually nonexistent. Thus, while Sendero Luminoso and the narcotics traffickers work together to achieve their goals, the forces of law and order are deadlocked in a senseless power struggle that further alienates the populace, playing into the hands of Sendero. In the process, the citizens of the region are becoming further estranged from the state.

As of late 1989, Army General Alberto Arciniega took charge of his office as political and military chief of the Huallaga region. His style for fighting the insurgency is quite different from his predecessors'. General Arciniega's policy seems to be directed at gaining the hearts and the minds of the coca growers in an effort to reduce the social base of Sendero Luminoso. He maintains that the traffickers, not the peasants, are the criminals. His policy has generated controversy as he is perceived to be interfering with narcotics control in the area. General Arciniega has gained support from some of Peru's intellectuals who believe his approach to be the most effective way to counter Sendero in the Huallaga region.[73] Yet the narcoterrorist alliance has still not been recognized, and the interservice rivalries have not ceased.

7

Conclusion

Sendero Luminoso is possibly the most violent, vindictive, and elusive terrorist insurgency in the Western Hemisphere. Well organized and self-sustaining, it follows a revolutionary strategy under a unified command. Sendero's intellectual foundation – Abimael Guzmán's fusion of Marx, Lenin, Mao, and Mariátegui – bolsters the movement's impact on the ever-growing numbers of Peruvians under its influence. Guzmán's vision of Peru as filtered through the most radical Communist ideology, "Gonzalism," represents a strike for underclass nationalism in Peru. If Sendero is to be countered effectively, both the ideological roots and the overall strategy of the movement must be better understood and acknowledged in Peru, in the rest of Latin America, and in the Western world.

The popular war waged by Sendero Luminoso is destroying Peru, as Sendero Luminoso razes anything that stands for the "bourgeoisie state" or the "hated quality of the enemy." The insurgency has systematically paralyzed industrial production, destroyed essential infrastructure (electric pylons, railroads, roads, and bridges, as well as Peru's oil pipeline), and halted desperately needed development projects. Sendero Luminoso has erased the authority of the state in certain areas by attacking police and military posts and killing police and military officers by cruel and grotesque means. It has executed elected officials and candidates, causing a chain of resignations and vacancies.[1] All democratic processes within areas under Sendero control have been disrupted, and electoral processes have been seriously hampered.

Sendero has capitalized well on the woes of the government and the country's collapsed economy. Sendero points quickly to democracy as the taproot of Peru's plight, mocking the impotence and incompetence of the government in providing the nation with basic services, a reasonably stable level of purchasing power, and tolerably secure living and working conditions. The threat of the Sendero challenge to the state is greater, however, than the present dire state of the Peruvian economy.[2]

If Guzmán's proposed system of order, as implemented by Sendero Luminoso, were ever to be imposed, Peru would be the seat of the most radical Communist regime since the Khmer Rouge. Sendero perceives the Peruvian revolution in an international context as a step toward the global Communist revolution that it anticipates will eventually sweep the world. Ironically, in the face of the collapse of the Communist system in Eastern Europe, and the end of one-party rule in the Soviet Union, Sendero considers itself the "beacon of world revolution" and endorses one-party dictatorship.

Sendero's stance may initially appear paradoxical in light of the movement's heavy nationalistic emphasis, but it must also be considered in a Latin American context. Sendero Luminoso seeks to unify the entire "Andean nation" (an entity it defines vaguely in terms of a shared racial and cultural heritage) against the existing exploitative and divisive state structures. Countries that neighbor Peru could well lend themselves to the Sendero approach, as all suffer, to varying degrees, from faltering governmental and economic performance. Already evidence has been found to suggest a link between Sendero Luminoso and insurgent movements in Bolivia.[3] Bolivia is particularly ripe for infiltration; in Bolivia, as in Peru, some sectors of the population now depend almost entirely upon coca production for their livelihood. The Bolivian "coca community," already provoked by U.S.-backed coca-eradication programs, is dangerously volatile and susceptible to Sendero influence. Sendero has penetrated northern Argentina; it staged a meeting in Tucumán in April 1989, as announced by the secretary of the Argentinian National Security Council.[4] It is believed that Sendero seeks to control the Corredor Salteño-Jujeño, a territory connecting Argentina with the Bolivian Chaco (in Salta, the departments of General San Martín and Orán; in Jujuy, the departments of Ledesma and Santa Bárbara).[5] According to its doctrine, Sendero Luminoso may also be seeking to expand north into Ecuador.

The emergence of narcoterrorism had deepened Sendero Luminoso's threat and the Peruvian government's dilemma. Protected by Senderistas, the drug network has created an efficient power base in the Upper Huallaga Valley from which it sustains an ever-increasing supply of cocaine paste to international trafficking syndicates. Because the alliance has created what amounts to a "state-within-a-state," geopolitical control of the region has been almost completely wrested from the hands of the Peruvian government. Multiple efforts by the government, many in conjunction with U.S. agencies, have served only to alienate the local people and fuel perceptions of official ineptitude. As of 1989, with the sovereign power of the state severely compromised in the Upper Huallaga, the situation shows no signs of abating. Given the huge sums of money that narcoterrorism has placed in the hands of growers, traffickers, and insurgents, the alliance threatens to erode the stability of U.S. allies in Peru, Colombia, Ecuador, and Brazil, as well as throughout Latin America.

Solutions for insurgent problems are, by nature, difficult to propose. In the case of Sendero Luminoso, the intricacies of the predicament and the degree of Sendero's penetration into the masses make the task particularly daunting. The combined socioeconomic, political, historical, and cultural conflicts that have allowed the movement to achieve its current prominence must be resolved if Sendero Luminoso is to be overcome. The experience of the past few years has demonstrated that raw military force will not successfully counter the insurgency.

Unquestionably, a democracy, with all its imperfections, remains the best solution for Peru. But Peru's fledgling democratic order must mature into one that more fully incorporates all Peruvians into a more just socioeconomic and political system. In countering Sendero propaganda, the Peruvian government should make it clear that Sendero Luminoso, for all its rhetoric, does not offer genuine solutions to Peru's grave social and economic problems.

Why have the counterinsurgency operations of the Peruvian government failed completely? As of early 1990, Sendero Luminoso has more power and influence than ever before. The government not only lacks a comprehensive national plan to overcome Sendero, but also misunderstands the intrinsic character of the movement. Army General Sinesio Jarama, who once presided over the Joint Chiefs of Staff, pointed out in a January 1989 interview that "government authorities have never studied in depth the ideological foundations of Sendero Luminoso to understand where the movement wants to go, or its procedures for fighting—politically, militarily, economically, and psychologically—to grasp the movement's political objectives."[6] As a result, he continues, "At no point has there been designed a nationally integrated anti-subversive strategy that, as an end, makes all of the state's forces of power and all of society's organizations converge."[7]

Sendero's Maoist political agenda of a revolution rising from the people rather than being imposed on them has gone almost completely unrecognized. Instead, the movement has been treated as an insurrection similar to the *foquista* Luís de la Puente Uceda uprising experienced by Peru in the mid-1960s (primarily a student initiative) or to Che Guevara's movement. The government has thus reacted to Sendero's initiatives with a purely military approach. Thousands of innocent victims have been killed or maimed, and thousands more have been turned to the insurrection. Violence has perpetuated violence and created despair as men and women see their lives and their families torn asunder.

The government's promises of economic assistance and development have gone unfulfilled. In the few cases where the state has allocated funds for projects of this category, monetary allotments have been insufficient and execution has been poor. The international community has also been sluggish in recognizing the threat to Peru and responding accordingly, although, in all fairness, this response stems in part from President García's unwillingness to work with the International Monetary Fund (IMF). Earlier in the 1980s, however, President Belaúnde's efforts to counter the insurrection with irrigation projects and development in Ayacucho were hampered by the IMF's insistence on austerity measures and by other problems facing the Belaúnde government. In short, a realistic economic counteroffensive has never been fully attempted.

Any effective counterinsurgency policy must begin by addressing the seriousness of Peru's economic situation. The nation's economic deterioration must be stopped. Inflation reached 1,722 percent in 1988 and 2,775 percent in 1989. It is not expected to abate in 1990.[8] Under such conditions, many people turn to the insurrection out of desperation, rather than ideological conviction.

The Peruvian government must develop a comprehensive counterinsurgency strategy that integrates all sectors of government and society. A strong educational push at all levels – primary, secondary, and university – would counter Sendero's propaganda efforts and bolster faith in democratic processes and institutions. Within the private sector, all civic organizations and businesses should take the initiative in giving members, associates, employees, and the population at large a realistic picture of the insurgency and stressing its implications for the nation. Alarm about the danger from Sendero Luminoso must be raised in an effort to unite all elements of Peruvian society in effective resistance.

The police and armed forces need crucial tactical training in counterinsurgency techniques and operations that do not endanger and abuse the population. Engagements initiated within the past few years have demonstrated that the wielding of military force alone is counterproductive in curbing the insurgency. A more refined plan of action is needed if the military is to be effective in protecting national security. Furthermore, government forces should be furnished with the equipment necessary to carry out counterinsurgency operations—for example, radios, radar, helicopters, and infrared equipment.

To dismantle the narcoterrorist alliance now established in the Upper Huallaga Valley, Peruvian military and law enforcement agencies need to overcome damaging interservice rivalries and formulate a long-term design for government presence in the region. Strict air control, aided by radar patrol planes and helicopters, could lessen the huge amounts of cocaine paste that are removed from the area daily. Eradication has received much attention in recent months as a possible solution. Short of aerial spraying (an option that entails notable environmental hazards), this plan is realistically unfeasible; if aerial spraying were implemented, however, the explosive political consequences would have to be taken into account.

In any case, an intensive crop-substitution program should be initiated for the Huallaga Valley. Such a project is already in the pilot stage in Santa Lucía in the Tocache area, where the Ministry of Agriculture and the National Planning Institute, in coordination with the DEA, have created a village—complete with a church, a school, and a sports field—that is surrounded by alternative crop fields (20,000 hectares).[9] Although this program is still in beginning stages, it is an important step in a new direction.

Narcoterrorism must be aggressively countered with a comprehensive multilateral strategy. At present, the Peruvian government simply lacks the economic and political capability to deal with this problem on its own: it is a new and highly complex alliance for which the Peruvian government is completely unprepared. Moreover, because this problem is international in scope, it particularly deserves a serious multilateral approach.

In the international arena, Peru should consult with its neighbors—Bolivia, Argentina, and Ecuador—about concerted action against Sendero and its offshoots. International cooperation between the Andean states and Western countries, particularly the United States, would enhance the likelihood of progress against Sendero Luminoso.

The Peruvian national elections of April 1990 did not grant a clear popular mandate to a single candidate or political association, leaving Congress without a majority and necessitating a runoff between the two leading presidential candidates. Mario Vargas Llosa and Alberto Fujimori, the presidential candidates, both embraced free-market ideas. Before the June 1990 runoff, however, Mr. Fujimori's plan of government was still relatively vague.

The new Peruvian administration that takes office in July 1990 has the opportunity to design and implement a comprehensive strategy, regrasp the reins of national power, and regain international credibility. New political alliances must be forged, rendering the future of the Peruvian political situation even more unforeseeable. A key factor in this political scenario are the independent voters—people who are disenchanted with the traditional parties and who could endorse either candidate.

As demonstrated by the 1990 electoral process, the Peruvian people, in the face of the Sendero challenge, have proven sufficiently brave to vote, even in areas of heavy Sendero presence. Their electoral participation reflects a vital surge of support for democracy as the cornerstone of the country's renewal.[10] But the new Peruvian administration faces an arduous task. The Sendero challenge will not disappear; further, it stands to gain from any weaknesses in either presidential hopeful. The postelection period is critical. The policies put in place by the government, and support for them from the international community, will be decisive for Peru's political and economic survival in the 1990s.

Notes

Chapter 1

1. Peru's 20 leftist political organizations in 1975 were as follows:

Communist Party of Peru – Unity (Partido Comunista del Perú – Unidad or PCP-U)

Communist Party of Peru – Red Flag (Partido Comunista del Perú – Bandera Roja or PCP-BR)

Communist Party of Peru – Marxist-Leninist (Partido Comunista del Perú – Marxista Leninista or PCP-ML)

Communist Party of Peru – Sendero Luminoso (Partido Comunista del Perú – Sendero Luminoso or PCP-SL)

Communist Party of Peru – Red Fatherland (Partido Comunista del Perú – Patria Roja or PCP-PR)

Communist Party of Peru – Red Star (Partido Comunista del Perú – Estrella Roja or PCP-ER)

National Liberation Front (Frente Nacional de Liberación or FLN)

Revolutionary Vanguard (Vanguardia Revolucionaria or VR)

Revolutionary Vanguard – Political Military (Vanguardia Revolucionaria – Político Militar or VR-PM)

Laborers' Revolutionary Marxist Party (Partido Obrero Marxista Revolucionario or POMR)

Communist League (Liga Comunista or LC)

International Socialist Party (Partido Socialista Internacionalista or PSI)

Revolutionary Communist Party (Partido Revolucionario Comunista or PCR)

Revolutionary Left Movement – Fourth Stage (Movimiento de Izquierda Revolucionaria – Cuarta Etapa or MIR-CE)

Revolutionary Left Movement – Reconstruction Tendency (Movimiento de Izquierda Revolucionaria – Tendencia por la reconstrucción or MIR-TR)

Marxist Circle of Proletarian Opposition (Círculo Marxista de Oposición Proletaria or CMOP)

Revolutionary Left Front (Frente de Izquierda Revolucionaria or FIR)

Workers' Socialist Party (Partido Socialista de los Trabajadores or PST)

National Liberation Army (Ejército de Liberación Nacional or ELN)

Laborers' Revolutionary Party – Trotsky (Partido Obrero Revolucionario – Trotskista or POR-T)

2. Luis Arce Borja, ed., "La entrevista del siglo," *El Diario*, July 1988.

3. Banco Central de Reserva del Perú, *Mapa de Pobreza del Perú 1981*, prepared by the Gerencia de Investigación Económica, Subgerencia de Ingreso y Producto (Lima: Banco Central de Reserva del Perú, December 1986), 24.

4. Viceroy Baltazar de la Cueva y Enríquez founded the university on July 3, 1677 under King Carlos II of Spain with the approval of Pope Innocent XI. Two centuries later, President Miguel Iglesias closed it on January 31, 1885 as a result of economic hardships brought to the nation by the War of the Pacific. UNSCH was reopened under President Manuel Prado on April 24, 1957 and began classes on July 3, 1959.

5. The General Studies program was a two-year, fixed sequence of courses required of all students seeking a degree. It was in many ways comparable to the introductory liberal arts courses taught at many U.S. universities.

6. The alliance between Sendero and the Student Revolutionary Front is well documented by Piedad Pareja Pflucker in *Terrorismo y Sindicalismo en Ayacucho (1980)* (Lima: Empresa Editora Ital Perú S.A., 1981), 78–81.

7. See David Scott Palmer, "The Origins and Evolution of

Sendero Luminoso," *Comparative Politics* 18, no. 2 (January 1986): 127–146; idem, "The Sendero Luminoso Rebellion in Rural Peru," in *Latin American Insurgencies,* ed. Georges Fauriol (Washington, D.C.: Center for Strategic and International Studies, 1985), 67–97; and Cynthia McClintock, "Sendero Luminoso: Peru's Maoist Guerrillas," in *Problems of Communism* 32 (September–October 1983): 19–34.

8. Data from Instituto Nacional de Estadística. Underemployment is a state in which an individual is unable to find legitimate employment commensurate with his ability or education (for example, a civil engineer who cannot find employment in engineering and is therefore self-employed informally as a taxi driver).

9. Instituto Nacional de Estadística, *Perú: Compendio Estadístico 1987* (Lima: Instituto Nacional de Estadística, May 1988), 299. For an analysis of the informal economy in Peru, see Hernando De Soto, *The Other Path,* trans. June Abbott (New York: Harper and Row, 1989).

10. Félipe MacGregor, Marcial Rubio, and Alejandro San Martín, eds., *Siete ensayos sobre la violencia en el Perú* (Lima: Asociación Peruana de Estudios para la Paz, 1987), preface.

11. Ibid.

Chapter 2

1. José Carlos Mariátegui, *Siete Ensayos de Interpretación de la Realidad Peruana,* 7th ed. (Lima: Empresa Editora Amauta, 1959). English edition: José Carlos Mariátegui, *Seven Interpretative Essays on Peruvian Reality,* trans. Marjory Urquidi (Austin: University of Texas Press, 1971).

2. Mariátegui, Autobiographical Notes, in *Siete Ensayos de Interpretación de la Realidad Peruana.* These notes are actually selected quotations from a letter written by Mariátegui to Enrique Espinoza (Samuel Glusberg) and published in the May 1930 issue of *La Vida Literaria,* Buenos Aires, a magazine edited by Espinoza.

3. Jesús Chavarría, *José Carlos Mariátegui and the Rise of Modern Peru 1890–1930* (Albuquerque: University of New Mexico Press, 1979), 59. For additional information on Mariátegui, his life, and his writings, see John M. Baines, *Revolution in Peru:*

Mariátegui and the Myth (Tuscaloosa, Ala.: University of Alabama Press, 1972).

4. Chavarría, *José Carlos Mariátegui*, 65. Henri Barbusse wrote *Clarté* (*Clarity*) in 1919 (Paris). He stressed the importance of the intellectuals in educating the masses, so that they could be mobilized toward revolution. Baines, *Revolution in Peru*, 34. Barbusse proposed that the task of the revolutionaries was to complete the destruction of the bourgeois state (ibid., 31).

5. Gabriele D'Annunzio, leader of the Italian Socialists, arrived in power at the time that Mariátegui went to Italy in the early 1920s (ibid., 38). Pierro Gobetti, the radical Marxist intellectual whom Mariátegui met in 1920, influenced Mariátegui deeply and was his "constant point of reference" (ibid., 69).

6. Chavarría, *José Carlos Mariátegui*, 66.

7. *Claridad*, the journal under the direction of Mariátegui, in its first issue featured a front-page article on Lenin as a salute to "the memory of the great Russian teacher and agitator," in the name of the "organized vangard of the proletariat, youth and revolutionary intellectuals of Peru." See Chavarría, *José Carlos Mariátegui*, 79.

8. Mariátegui, *Siete Ensayos de Interpretación*.

9. Manuel Gonzáles Prada inaugurated a generation of *indigenistas* with his concern for the Indian masses. He exalted the Inca heritage and very likely served as the departure point for Mariátegui. His concern, however, was social in nature, not political; it was Mariátegui who introduced Marxism to the issue. These seven essays were included in Mariátegui's work: "Outline of Economic Evolution," "The Problem of the Indian," "The Problem of Land," "Public Education," "The Religious Factor," "Regionalism and Centralism," and "Literature on Trial."

10. Baines, *Revolution in Peru*, 5.

11. Ibid.

12. Mariátegui, *Siete Ensayos de Interpretación*, 45; Mariátegui, *Seven Interpretative Essays* (trans. Urquidi), 35. In addition to this quotation, this book is the source for much of Mariátegui's understanding of and appreciation for the Inca Empire.

13. Ibid.

14. The Spaniards' two primary attractions to the New World were precious metals and religious dominance.

15. Mariátegui, *Siete Ensayos de Interpretación*, 45. Mariátegui writes on the period of the Spanish conquest and coloniza-

tion in painstaking detail, describing the destruction of Peruvian society: the carnage of the Indians and their forced labor in the gold and silver mines under the *Obrajes* system (which amounted to slavery, not servitude), and the Spanish legacy of the *latifundia*, not as the *hacienda* per se but as the socioeconomic system of omnipresent landed classes and the servitude of the Indians.

16. Mariátegui writes that the term *gamonalismo* does not refer only to the landed classes, but rather describes a complex phenomenon. *Gamonalismo* comprehends a large hierarchy of state functionaries, intermediaries, agents, and parasites. Under this system literate Indians transformed themselves into agents of exploitation against their own race, putting themselves at the service of *gamonalismo*. Large landowners exercised political hegemony in government and the state. See the preface written by Mariátegui for Luis Valcarcel's "Tempestad en los Andes," in Mariátegui, *Siete Ensayos de Interpretación*, 34.

17. Mariátegui constantly explained that communism had not ceased to exist in the Indian communities and wrote, "We proclaim that at this moment in our history, it is not possible to effectively be nationalistic and revolutionary without being socialist." Ibid., 34.

18. It is important to note that even though Guzmán refers to his party as "Marxist-Leninist," it is opposed to Soviet communism and not affiliated with the Communist International.

19. Luis Arce Borja, "La entrevista del siglo," *El Diario*, July 1988, pp. 84–85.

20. Baines, *Revolution in Peru*, 103.

21. Instigating a revolution in Peru was exactly what Mariátegui had hoped for – to this possibility he ultimately devoted his life and all his writings.

22. José María Salcedo, "Con Sendero en Lurigancho," *Quehacer* 39 (February–March 1986): 65.

23. Gustavo Gorriti, "Gonzalismo y fanatismo," *Caretas* 716 (September 27, 1982): 34.

24. Gustavo Gorriti, "Sendero en el Frontón," *Caretas* 715 (September 9, 1982): 65.

25. Arce Borja, "La entrevista de siglo," 53–55.

26. Laura Puertas, "Instruído para matar," *Caretas* 1008 (May 30, 1988): 32. In this article, Puertas interviews Isidoro Nunja García, a Sendero commander.

27. Gorriti, "Sendero en el Frontón," 66.

28. Gordon H. McCormick, "The Shining Path and Peruvian Terrorism," *Inside Terrorist Organizations*, ed. David C. Rappoport (New York: Columbia University Press, 1988), 112.

29. Mao Zedong, *On New Democracy* (Beijing: Foreign Languages Press, 1960). This piece was written in 1940.

30. Personal interview with Professors Guo Meifeng and Jian Wenguang, March 8, 1989 (Davidson College, Davidson, North Carolina).

31. Roger Mercado, *Sendero Luminoso*, 3rd ed. (Lima: La Mano Izquierda Ediciones Latinoamericanas, 1988), 136.

32. Puertas, "Instruído para matar," 31.

33. Arce Borja, "La entrevista del siglo," 70.

34. Decree Law 17716 of June 24, 1969.

35. The value of the land, as determined by the government, was to be paid back to the hacienda owners in government bonuses over a 20-year period.

36. Abimael Guzmán has termed this era "corporatist" because of the strong presence of the state in the entrepreneurial field. He claims the state attempted a corporatist reorganization of society.

Chapter 3

1. Gorriti, "Gonzalismo y fanatismo," 33.

2. See José Gonzáles, "Se despunta Sendero?" *Debate* 47 (November–December 1987): 33, for a map of Sendero presence in Peru. See also, Raúl Gonzáles, "El voto y la subversión," *Debate* 55 (March–May 1989): 16–17, which displays two maps of Peru, one of the zones in which Sendero has rooted itself and another of its areas of operation.

3. Sendero Luminoso, "Let Us Develop the Guerrilla War!" (March 1982), English translation by Colin Harding, *Communist Affairs* 3 (Guildford: Butterworth Scientific, 1984), 54. As the urban front has gained momentum, Sendero, much like other terrorist organizations, has begun to turn to the media to propagate the movement and its effectiveness.

4. Luis Arce Borja, "Linea militar, Sendero y el Ejército Guerrillero Popular," *El Diario* (insert), January 6, 1988, p. VIII.

5. An example of how Sendero indoctrination is focusing on small children can be found in the spelling homework — *Presidente Gonzalo and lucha armada* (armed struggle) — given to children by

Senderistas in the shantytown of San Juan de Lurigancho in Lima. "Sendero capta adeptos entre niños," *Expreso*, February 3, 1989, p. 5.

6. These are official figures. Other sources estimate that inflation in the informal economy is between 300 and 500 percent greater. Inflation figures for 1988 from Roger Cohen, "Peru's Guerrillas Draw Support of Peasants in Coca-Rich Regions," *Wall Street Journal*, January 17, 1989, p. 1. Also, Desco, *Resumen Semanal*, no. 501 (January 5, 1989): 1. Inflation figures for 1989 from *El Comercio*, editorial, January 5, 1990, p. A2. Statistics for 1982 from David S. Palmer, "Peru," in *1983 Yearbook on International Communist Affairs*, ed. Robert Wesson (Stanford: Hoover Institution Press, 1983), 123.

7. Carlos Iván Degregori, *Sendero Luminoso*, 41–44.

8. See Instituto Nacional de Estadística, *Perú: Compendio Estadístico 1987*, p. 80, for a table on university students prepared by the Association of Higher Education (Asamblea Nacional de Rectores).

9. "[Forty] months after [President Alan García] swept to power amid a wave of optimism . . . [Peru] is effectively bankrupt, terrorism is rampant, and inflation is spiralling out of control . . . Peru is in danger of becoming the Lebanon of Latin America." Roger Cohen, "Survival of García's Peru, Bankrupt and Beset by Terrorism, Is Questioned," *Wall Street Journal*, December 6, 1988, p. A21.

10. César Rodríguez Rabanal explains the feelings of the migrants in the cities – the "not belonging." The personalities of urban migrants are fractured when the Andean culture loses ground and is negated and disvalued. César Rodríguez Rabanal and Franca Castelnuovo, "Sobre la dimensión psicosocial de la violencia en el Perú," in Félipe MacGregor, José Luis Rouillón, and Marcial Rubio, eds., *Siete ensayos sobre la violencia en el Perú* (Lima: APEP, 1987), 48.

11. Highland children quoted in Chavez-Toro, "Los hijos del terror," *Caretas* 963 (July 13, 1987): 37. A man in his late sixties, who has a store in a town that Sendero entered in 1988, gave this testimony: "When Sendero came to town they entered to my store and asked for supplies and I provided them. Then they called for a meeting in the plaza where they lectured us on President Gonzalo and the New Democratic Republic. After the meeting we had to say: ¡viva el Presidente Gonzalo!, ¡viva la Revolución! . . . I said

that too. . . . What else could I do? . . . Then the military came and wanted us to identify the Senderistas and who cooperated with them—Sendero has a thousand eyes and ears. Sendero came several times and I gave them all they wanted . . . to refuse them will be to die." The man's identity is protected for security reasons. (Author's personal notes.)

12. See José Gonzáles, "Se despunta Sendero?" 33. For information about areas in which Sendero has taken root and operates, see Raúl Gonzáles, "El voto y la subversión," 16–17.

13. These damages to the Peruvian economy were estimated at U.S. $10 billion ($10,000 million) by Prime Minister Armando Villanueva in his presentation to the Peruvian congress on March 10, 1989. With the continuing of sabotage attacks, these figures have undoubtedly climbed.

14. Among the many international companies that have suffered losses at the hands of Sendero are Bayer and Nissan. A Bayer acrylic fiber factory was destroyed in May 1983, and a Nissan factory was attacked in November 1987.

15. For information on downed pylons, see "En los últimos 10 años fueron derribadas 1,205 torres," *Expreso*, January 14, 1990, p. 13. ElectroPeru's press release contains statistics on damages to the electric sector from 1980 to 1989. See "En 1989 derribaron 335 torres," *Expreso*, January 5, 1990, p. 8. In 1989, the insurgency downed the greatest number of towers (335) during the period. For additional information on the damages to the electric sector, see "Tiempos de tinieblas," *Caretas* (December 12, 1988): 45–48. The lack of electricity affecting Lima and major cities deepened during 1989 and shows no signs of abating in early 1990. "Seguirá restringida la energía," *Expreso*, January 14, 1990, p. 13.

16. Charles Maechling, "Handcuffing Terrorism," *Foreign Service Journal* 64, no. 1 (January 1987): 22.

17. Estimate provided by the Ministry of the Interior. Interview with Ministry of the Interior official, Lima, August 1988. In July 1989, the Peruvian police reported 14,209 deaths for the period 1980–1989. The number is accounted for as follows: 1,057 police and armed forces personnel, 7,573 terrorists, and 5,579 civilians. "Mas de 14 mil muertos por violencia terrorista," *Expreso*, July 13, 1989.

18. David G. Hubbard, "Terrorism Is Criminal Activity," *Terrorism* (Opposing Viewpoints Series), ed. Bonnie Szumski (St. Paul, Minnesota: Greenhaven Press, 1986), 30.

19. Sendero Luminoso, "Let Us Develop the Guerrilla War!" 50.

20. "Muerte de un oficial," *Caretas* 904 (May 12, 1986): 20–25, 80.

21. "Otra vez," *Caretas* 927 (October 20, 1986): 26.

22. The assassination of U.S. citizen Constantine Gregory in Sincos near Huancayo, department of Junín, June 14, 1988, is a lamentable example, as are the assassinations of French researchers Thomas Pelissier and Corine Seguin on December 3, 1988. See "El americano inocente," *Caretas* 1011 (June 20, 1988): 38–39 for the former and "Dos franceses y tres peruanos asesinados," *Expreso*, December 7, 1988, p. 12, for the latter. British citizen Edward Bartley was killed in Olleros, department of Ancash, on May 25, 1989. See *Expreso*, June 10, 1989, p. 12.

23. Abilio Arroyo and Gustavo Gorriti, "Masacre en Cochas," *Caretas* 923 (September 29, 1986): 45–47, 72.

24. On the destruction of 17 communities (5,000 families), see ibid., 72. On the five-week period of attacks in 1988, see "Tumbas de Ancos, Sendero y la matanza indiscriminada," *Caretas* (January 18, 1988): 80.

25. Stuart Schram, *The Political Thought of Mao Tse Tung* (New York: Praeger Publishing, 1963), 287. This work also provides a complete description of Mao's military thought and strategy (pp. 265–293).

26. Sendero Luminoso, "Let Us Develop the Guerrilla War!" 50.

27. Luis Arce Borja, "Linea militar," VI.

28. Ibid., VIII.

29. Ibid., VII.

30. Ibid., VIII, XI.

31. Besides the well-known killings of policemen to seize their weapons, an illustrative example of an attack on the military can be found in the systematic strike on military cars transporting troops. One of them occurred in Aucayacu, Huánuco at the end of 1988. In the wake of the insurgency's destruction of seven military vehicles, local police and military resorted to travel in civilian cars. On November 21, 1988, 22 soldiers and several civilians boarded two pickup trucks to be transported from the village Ramal de Aspusana to their base in Aucayacu. While in transit, the road exploded underneath the first pickup truck, and the impact made the second pickup truck turn over. The detonation of

approximately 100 kilograms of dynamite sent pieces of machinery and bits of bodies flying high into the air. The Senderistas opened fire on the survivors in the second truck, leaving no survivors. Jimmy Torres, "Aucayacu, territorio de combate," *Caretas* (November 28, 1988), pp. 30–31, 39. Another grotesque attack on a military vehicle was perpetuated in the heart of Lima, against the guard of the president, the Húsares de Junín battalion. A bus carrying 27 guards was moving in the direction of the presidential palace, at its scheduled time, when it slowed down because of traffic interference. Suddenly, from another vehicle, dynamite was tossed through the windows and underneath the bus. It exploded, causing a dantesque scenario, wherein pieces of bodies and machinery littered the street as five guards were killed and 14 were gravely injured. "Emboscada," *Caretas* 1060 (June 5, 1989): 80–83.

32. A military official said: "[We and the soldiers] live under constant tension, which Senderistas do not experience because they are the ones that attack us and then 'disappear.'" Torres, "Aucayacu, territorio de combate," 39.

33. Arce Borja, "Linea militar," VIII.

34. "Cuenta atteradora," *Caretas* (May 19, 1981): 44. Ministry of Interior official statistics for terrorist attacks (1985-1987) are as follows: 1985 – 1310, 1986 – 1715, and 1987 – 1623. Instituto Nacional de Estadística, *Peru: Compendio Estadístico 1987*, p. 372. These figures are the result of terrorist activity throughout the nation.

35. Puertas, "Instruído para matar," 32.

36. Ibid.

37. Testimony of a witness. Author's notes. Identity not disclosed at the request of the source.

38. On June 17, 1989, 16 electric towers were downed by Sendero Luminoso, plunging major urban centers of the nation (including Lima and coastal cities from Ica to Chiclayo) into a power blackout. The towers were located in the highland area of Piñascocha. This incident alone is daily costing ElectroPeru between U.S. $200,000-400,000 in repairs and emergency provisions. "Derriban 16 torres de energía en el centro," *Nacional* (Lima), June 17, 1989, p. 14.

Chapter 4

1. Puertas, "Instruído para matar," 28.

2. Raúl Gonzáles, "Las conferencias senderistas," *Quehacer*, August 30, 1984, pp. 19–20; and "La cuarta guerra," *Caretas* (September 2, 1985), 24-A.

3. See Sandra L. Woy-Hazleton, "Peru," in *1988 Yearbook on Communist Affairs* (Stanford, Calif.: Hoover Institution Press, 1988), 118.

4. Puertas, "Instruído para matar," 30.

5. See also, "Sendero urbano," *Caretas* 947 (March 23, 1987): 12.

6. "Organos de fachada," *Caretas* 947 (March 23, 1987): 16. See also, DIRCOTE police reports.

7. This information was gathered from documents seized as a result of Osmán Morote's capture.

8. "El Socorro de Sendero," *Caretas* (January 11, 1988): 14. See also, "Sicóloga de Hospital Policial es senderista," *Expreso*, December 30, 1987, p. 18.

9. José María Salcedo, "Con Sendero en Lurigancho," *Quehacer*, February–March 1982, p. 64.

10. There is great secrecy surrounding the National Central Committee. Although there may be additional members of the cupola, their identities are not known. In particular, very little is known about Hildebrando Pérez.

11. Margi Calvo, Peralta Fiorella Montagne, and Laura Zambrano Padilla were the known secretaries of the Metropolitan Committee from 1983 to 1985. The metropolitan coordinator, Segundo Chávez Diaz, was also considered a member of the cupola before his capture and subsequent death in the Lurigancho prison uprising of June 19, 1986.

12. See chapter 1 for additional information regarding the FER and the rupture of the Communist Party of Peru.

13. Sendero en París: El ultimo tango," *Caretas* 966 (August 3, 1987): 38–40; "Carta de París," *Caretas* 681 (January 18, 1982): 14.

14. "La captura de meche," *Caretas* 810 (July 30, 1984).

15. An Instituto Nacional Penitenciario report states that Laura Zambrano Padilla was as of February 1989 incarcerated at the Miguel Castro Castro prison in Lima.

16. Stuart R. Schram, ed., *Quotations from Mao Tse-Tung* (New York: Bantam Books, Inc., 1967), 169–170.

17. José Gonzáles, "Sendero de mujeres," *Sí*, April 6, 1987, p. 83.

18. The Peruvian Constitution of 1979 (Article 2) affirms the equality of gender under the law, but tradition persists in certain sectors of the populace.

Chapter 5

1. *Caretas* 648 (May 19, 1981) published a map (labeled as "Geografia del terror") with the numbers of terrorist attacks per department. The highest number of terrorist incidents occurred in Ayacucho (83) and Lima (81).

2. Decree Laws 19049 of 1971 and 20828 of 1974.

3. This Constitution of 1979 entered into effect July 28, 1980 — at the same time President Belaúnde took office. The earlier Constitution of 1933 was also drafted in accordance with human rights, freedom of expression, and freedom of political association. Following the October 1968 coup d'etat of General Juan Velasco Alvarado, it was replaced by El Estatuto Revolucionario de las Fuerzas Armadas (which did not recognize these freedoms) and remained in effect until 1980.

4. The Congress of Peru, in accordance with Article 188 of the Constitution, passed Law 23230 of December 15, 1980, giving the executive the power to enact legislative decrees to update legislation passed by the military government since October 3, 1968.

5. Fourth, fifth, and sixth paragraphs of the opening section (*Considerando*) of Legislative Decree 46.

6. Decree Law 46, Article 1. It is important to note that this legal definition does not differentiate terrorism from sabotage and treats both as acts of terrorism.

7. Luis Roy Freyre, "Los fundamentos de la ley antiterrorista," *Revista del Foro* 68, no. 1 (January–June 1981): 152, cited in Felipe Villavicencio, *Delito Contra la Seguridad Publica: Delito de Terrorismo* (Lima: Editora Los Andes, 1981), 195. Luis Roy Freyre and Luis Bramont Arias were the authors of this law on terrorism.

8. Decree Law 46, Article 5 (first paragraph).

9. Ibid. (second paragraph).

10. Ibid., Article 6.

11. Ibid., Article 7.

12. Peruvian Constitution, Article 109.

13. The provision dictating the presence of a prosecutor from

the Public Ministry preexisted in the Law of the Public Ministry—Legislative Decree 52, Article 10 and Article 94, Disposition 1.

14. DIRCOTE experts analyzed the characters of the handwriting and concluded that these documents were written by Morote. See also, Laura Puertas, "Los papeles de Morote," *Caretas* 1012 (June 27, 1988): 10–14.

15. The text of the law says "to modify," but the text of the legal dispositions is different, having to do with express revocation rather than modification.

16. Law 24953, Article 283-C.

17. Ibid., Article 288-D (first section).

18. Ibid. (second section).

19. Often the only evidence that the judicial authorities had was the investigation by the police transcribed in a report document named "Atestado Policial." In most cases, these "Atestados" were insufficient and poorly substantiated. Also see "Procesos y sentencias," *Caretas* 782 (January 16, 1984).

20. The Peruvian Congress subsequently enacted Law 23414 on July 1, 1982, which mandated that all terrorist trials be held in the province of Lima. This measure was taken in the context of a massive Sendero attack on the Huamanga jail on March 2, 1982, in which 50 detained terrorist suspects were freed, among them Sendero leader Edith Lagos. For further reading on the Huamanga jail break, see Gustavo Gorriti, "Morir en Huamanga," *Caretas* 688 (March 8, 1982): 12–15.

21. Law 24700 of June 24, 1987.

22. For an illustration of the feelings of magistrates charged with judging cases of terrorism, see "Jueces Especiales," *Sí,* October 19, 1987, pp. 29–30; and "Jueces se abstienen," *Caretas* 1019 (August 15, 1988): 20–21.

23. For some of the verdicts, see Jimmy Torres, "Sentencias, mano dura," *Caretas* 996 (March 7, 1988).

24. Supreme Court Administrative Resolution 19-88 P-65. The issue was decided in the plenum of March 8, 1988.

25. "Miembros de Tribunal Especial, Seguro por Cien Mil Dolares Piden Para Juzgar a Morote," *Expreso,* June 8, 1989, p. 14.

26. For information regarding this Special Tribunal, see *Expreso,* June 10, 1989, p. 12; *Expreso,* June 8, 1989, p. 14; *El Comercio* (Lima), June 13, 1989, p. A8.

27. DIRCOTE was created as a division of the Peruvian Investigative Police (Policía de Investigación del Perú or PIP). Originally, it was known as DICOTE and was composed of 100 men, led by Colonel Héctor Agurto. The force was later granted Dirección status. Because it is known only as DIRCOTE in Peru, the author has preferred to use this designation throughout.

28. The Sinchis, an antisubversive brigade, was created in 1965 as a division of the Civil Guard to quell the Luis de la Puente Uceda and Héctor Béjar groups. The Llapan Aticcs squad was created at the same time as a division of the Republican Guard, also to counter subversive elements. Both terms are of Quechua origin; Sinchi signifies a brave warrior of the Inca Pachacutec and Llapan Attic signifies "one who is capable of everything." By the end of 1989, the García administration officially merged all police units into La Policía Nacional and placed its special forces under Dirección de Operaciones Especiales.

29. Peru's Constitution, Article 231, allows this state of exception in the case of perturbation of internal order or grave circumstances that affect the well-being of the nation. In this case, the constitutional guarantees related to liberty and personal security are suspended. The suspended guarantees (inviolability of residence and the liberty of assembly and travel) correspond to Dispositions 7, 9, and 10 of Article 2, and to Disposition 20-g, also of Article 2. Other constitutional guarantees are upheld.

30. See Gustavo Gorriti, "Entró el Ejército: Trágicos augurios," *Caretas* 729 (December 27, 1982): 23, 66.

31. As of August 1988, 36 provinces in 7 departments were under state-of-emergency status. Interview with Ministry of the Interior official, Ministry of the Interior, Lima, August 1988.

32. For additional information, see Americas Watch Committee, *Abdicating Democratic Authority: Human Rights in Peru* (New York: Americas Watch, October 1984), and Amnesty International, *Peru: Torture and Extrajudicial Executions* (New York: Amnesty International, August 1983).

33. Peruvian human rights organizations added their voices to the clamor, including the Instituto de Defensa Legal, Servicio de Derechos Humanos de la Comisión Episcopal de Acción Social, and the Colegio de Abogados de Lima.

34. Nelson Manrique cites Banco de datos de DESCO, "La guerra silenciosa," *Violencia y campesinado* (Lima: Instituto de Apoyo Agrario, 1985), 18–19.

35. "Los soles de guerra," *Caretas* 761 (August 15, 1983): 15. The figure cited in the text is a conversion of the 36.8 billion Peruvian *soles* that the government planned to invest. The dollar figure was obtained using a conversion rate of 1,300 *soles* per dollar, which was accurate as of March 1983. The irrigation projects were planned for Carajay, Masinga, Colca, Lucanas, and Parinacochas. Some agricultural and livestock programs were also to be implemented.

36. For additional information on the economic situation in Ayacucho and the other highland departments, see chapter 1.

37. Belaúnde implemented a program of economic austerity as dictated by the IMF. Thus, loans and other available funds were used more to service existing debts than for internal investment. These policies led to inflation in excess of 100 percent and a growth rate of a negative 6 percent. Woy-Hazleton, "Peru," in *1984 Yearbook of International Communist Affairs* (Stanford, Calif.: Hoover Institution Press, 1985), 165.

38. CONAPLAN—the National Government Plan Commission or Comisión Nacional de Plan de Gobierno of the APRA party.

39. See "Remezón militar," *Caretas* 869 (September 23, 1985): 23–24.

40. For an example of Sendero's ferocity and the Andean communities' lack of protection under military jurisdiction, see Gustavo Gorriti, "Pueblos inermes," *Caretas* (September 29, 1986): 45–46, 72.

41. Human rights violations continue to take place in the Andean departments of Ayacucho, Apurímac, and Huánuco. Organizations such as Amnesty International, Americas Watch, and others have documented the excesses of the military in depth. See Amnesty International, *Peru: Violations of Human Rights in the Emergency Zones* (New York: Amnesty International, August 1988), and Americas Watch, *Tolerating Abuses: Violations of Human Rights in Peru* (New York: Americas Watch, 1988).

Sources of information on Peru's state of emergency are as follows: 1988—interview with high official in the Ministry of Interior, Lima, August 1988; 1989—Joseph B. Treaster, "Rebels Step Up Killings in Peru to Disrupt Election," *New York Times*, October 26, 1989, p. A5.

42. For additional information on the peasant patrols or *rondas campesinas*, see Raúl Gonzáles, "Campesinos, ronderos, y

guerra antisubversiva," *Quehacer* 46 (April–May 1987): 72–79. Also, Carlos Iván Degregori, *Sendero Luminoso* (Lima: Instituto de Estudios Peruanos, 1988), Part 2, pp. 47–50, and Nelson Manrique, "La guerra silenciosa," in Alberto Flores Galindo and Nelson Manrique, *Violencia y campesinado* (Lima: Instituto de Apoyo Agrario, 1986).

43. The peasant patrol concept can be traced to the hacienda system. Landowners formed their own internal police within the borders of their estates to patrol the land and protect livestock.

44. *Comité de Defensa Civil* (Civil Defense Committee) was the official name given to the new peasant communities. They are more commonly referred to as *montoneras* (meaning a "heap" or "pile"); Sendero Luminoso has termed these communities *mesnadas* ("flock of sheep").

45. Gonzáles, "Campesinos," 76–79.

46. Degregori, *Sendero Luminoso*, 41.

47. Gonzáles, "Campesinos," 75–76.

48. Hugo Ned Alarcón, "Rumi Rumi, la masacre," *Caretas* (December 21, 1987). See also *Amnesty International, Report 1988* (New York: Amnesty International, 1988), 132.

49. Accounts abound in the Peruvian press on the activities of *rondas campesinas*, the ferocity with which Sendero attacks them, and their relationship with the government forces. See, for example, "Sendero vuelve a matar," *Caretas* (June 6, 1987): 70–71.

50. "El famoso Huayhuaco," *Caretas* (December 11, 1989), 37.

Chapter 6

1. Peter Nares, "Colombian Guerrillas' Drug Connections Crystallize in Shoot-Outs," *Wall Street Journal*, November 15, 1985, p. 31.

2. The UN released a report in June 1987 stating that drug production and trafficking are linked closely to the illegal arms trade and terrorism. Issued by the Vienna-based International Narcotics Board, the report notes that "these illegal activities are financed and masterminded by criminal organizations with links and accomplices in financial circles. . . . in certain regions, drug trafficking is closely interconnected with other major criminal activities, including trafficking in weapons, and is associated with subversion and terrorism." Elaine Sciolino, "U.N. Report

Links Drugs, Arms Trafficking and Terror," *New York Times*, January 13, 1987.

3. Gabriela Tarazona-Sevillano, "Deadly Alliance Threatens U.S. Allies," *Commercial Appeal*, Memphis, Tenn., May 12, 1988.

4. Gabriela Tarazona-Sevillano, "The Personality of the Shining Path and Narcoterrorism," seminar paper, Center for Strategic and International Studies (CSIS), Washington, D.C., February 29, 1988.

5. The first roads to penetrate the Huallaga region were built under the administrations of Oscar Benavides (1933–1939) and Manuel Prado (1939–1945). Within the region, the Huánuco–Tingo María road was built in 1926 and the Tingo María–Pucallpa road was built in 1946.

6. The *enganche* system involves a form of de facto labor contract in which the worker is hired temporarily to perform manual labor at a fixed payment for a predetermined amount of time (six months or a year). The contractor advances part of the money to the worker and takes care of his transportation, food, and shelter during the duration of the contract. In exchange the worker is obliged to work solely for the contractor.

7. Agreement 96/SF-PE of September 30, 1966, was signed by the InterAmerican Development Bank and the Corporación Financiera de Reforma Agraria (CORFIRA) of the Peruvian government.

8. Previously, agricultural activity was projected to occupy 59.2 percent of the project area, and the remaining 39.8 percent was to be devoted to livestock pasture. Instituto Nacional de Desarollo/Ministerio de Agricultura, "Análisis de la Situación de la Colonización Tingo María-Tocache-Campanilla," *Zona Agraria IX* (May 1974).

9. Ibid.

10. Ibid. p. 38.

11. Héctor Martínez (National University of San Marcos, Peru) presented a paper on this problem ("Los Estudios de la Migración y Ocupación Selvática Peruana") to the VII Reunión del Grupo de Trabajo sobre Migraciones de la Comisión de Población y Desarollo del Consejo Latinoamericano de Ciencias Sociales, Buenos Aires, August 25–29, 1980.

12. The destruction of forest resources has become increasingly serious as settlers slash and burn thousands of hectares every year to plant coca. To date, an estimated 800,000 hectares

of rain forest have been downed for coca cultivation, an amount roughly equal to the total agricultural area of the remainder of Peru. Enrique Zileri, "Coca y catástrofe," *Caretas* 996 (March 7, 1988): 23.

13. Other crops cultivated in the valley were tea, coffee, cacao, yellow corn, beans, bananas, and "yuca" (from the potato family). They did not offer stability to the economy because of the low prices paid by the merchant. Ministerio de Trabajo y Promoción Social, "Políticas de asentamiento y la economía campesina en el proceso colonizador de la Selva Alta," Moyobamba, Peru, January 25–27, 1984, p. 15.

14. Ibid., 15–17.

15. Lester Grinspoon and James B. Bakalar, *Cocaine: A Drug and Its Social Evolution* (New York: Basic Books, Inc., 1985), 12.

16. Ibid., 71–72.

17. Peruvian Decree Law 22095, February 21, 1978. Law of Repression of Illicit Drug Traffic (Ley de Represión del Tráfico Ilícito de Drogas).

18. Consejo Nacional de Población, Centro de Investigación y Promoción Amazónica, *Población y colonizacion en la Alta Amazonía Peruana* (Lima: CNP/CIPA, 1984), 31.

19. Decree Law 22927 of March 4, 1980, declared under the state of emergency (only for coca crop control) the departments of Huánuco and San Martín and the province of Coronel Portillo in the department of Loreto.

20. Decree Law 22926 of March 4, 1980.

21. Ministerio de Trabajo y Promoción Social, "Políticas de asentimiento y la economía campesina," 14.

22. The 1988 figure was taken from an interview with a high official in the Ministry of Interior, Lima, August 1988. Total for 1980 estimated from Peruvian Senate, Comisión Investigadora del Narcotráfico Report 981/82-S, Lima, May 28, 1982. The report states that Peru's total legal area of coca leaf production amounted to 17,862 hectares in 1982; at the same time, illegal area under coca cultivation was estimated at 50,000 hectares. The Huallaga region's illegal cultivation was thought to approximate 28,000 hectares.

23. Consejo Nacional de Población, *Población y colonización en la Alta Amazonía Peruana*, 31.

24. Alan Riding, "Rebels Disrupting Coca Eradication in Peru," *New York Times*, January 26, 1989, p. 6Y.

25. Tarazona-Sevillano, "Personality of Shining Path," 12.

26. Raúl Gonzáles, "Coca y subversión en el Huallaga," *Quehacer* 48 (September–October 1987): 67.

27. Ibid.

28. Ibid.

29. Zileri, "Coca y catástrofe," 42.

30. Most of the information in this paragraph came from an interview with a high official in the Ministry of the Interior, Lima, August 1988. (Names not disclosed for security reasons.)

31. Comité Multisectoral de Control de Drogas, *Plan Nacional de Prevención y Control de Drogas — Mediano Plazo 1986–1990* (Lima: Comité Multisectoral de Control de Drogas, 1986), 84. This study states that each metric ton of coca leaves produces seven kilograms of cocaine hydrochloride. One kilogram of cocaine hydrochloride is extracted from three kilograms of cocaine paste (Pasta Básica de Cocaína or PBC), 21. Thus, 21 kilograms of cocaine paste may be extracted from each ton of coca leaves.

32. Interview with Ministry of the Interior official, Lima, August 1988.

33. The actual price of cocaine to wholesalers is a topic of great speculation and is subject to wide fluctuations. In a *Nightline* report of summer 1988, Ted Koppel stated that the price per kilo was dropping while quality had greatly improved. Koppel set the per kilo price at U.S. $10,000–20,000. The conservative figure has been used for this document's calculations.

The author's estimates for profits from the production and sale of Peruvian cocaine are calculated for 1988 as follows:

200,000	hectares of coca fields
×2	metric tons of coca leaves, processed & refined into cocaine, that reach U.S. eventually
400,000	metric tons of leaves
×7	kilograms of cocaine hydrochloride per metric ton
2,800,000	kilograms of cocaine hydrochloride
×10,000	U.S. $ per kilogram
$28,000,000,000	profit for 1988

34. Peru's 1987 GNP was U.S. $36,076 billion (Banco Central de Reserva del Peru, February 1989).

35. Peru's 1987 earnings from copper were U.S. $0.514 billion (Banco Central de Reserva del Peru, February 1989).

36. Alejandro Deustua, *El narcotráfico y el interés nacional* (Lima: Centro Peruano de Estudios Internacionales, 1987), 38–39.

37. Gonzáles, "Coca y subversión en el Huallaga," 64.

38. Interview with Ministry of the Interior official, Lima, August 1988.

39. Data on Peru's per capita income from World Bank, *World Development Report* (New York: Oxford University Press, July 1986), 180 (table 1: "Basic Indicators"). Farmers who plant a legal crop are even charged by middlemen an interest rate of 10 to 12 percent on the loan given to plant that crop. The merchant benefits not only from the low prices he pays for the crop, but from the interest of the loan, leaving the peasant with no surplus. Ministerio de Trabajo y Promoción Social, *Políticas de asentimiento y la economía campesina,* 17.

40. Eduardo Bedoya, "Intensificación y degradación en los sistemas agrícolas de la Selva Alta: El caso del Alto Huallaga," in Eduardo Bedoya, Jane Collins, and Michael Painter, *Estrategias productivas y recursos naturales en la Amazonía* (Lima: Centro de Investigación y Promoción Amazónica, 1986), 76. In Tingo María, the average family plot is approximately 19.5 hectares, while in Tocache-Uchiza, family holdings average 30.07 hectares. It should be remembered that not all of this land is necessarily in cultivation at once, nor is it all dedicated to coca.

41. For example, the assault to the Civil Guard post in Uchiza on May 31, 1987, where nine policemen and four civilians were killed (Jorge Chavez Morales, "Al día siguiente," *Sí*, June 8, 1987, pp. 2–10); also, the ambush to the military convoy by Senderistas (aided by local people) on the road from Tingo María to Monzón, July 3, 1988. Thirteen military personnel lost their lives. Interview with an official at the National Attorney's Office, Lima, August 1988.

42. See "Alianza de narcotraficantes y terroristas: ¡Toman Tocache!" *Sí*, June 1, 1987, pp. 76–85.

43. Tarazona-Sevillano, "Personality of Shining Path," 14.

44. Roger Cohen, "Cocaine Rebellion," *Wall Street Journal,* January 17, 1989, p. 1.

45. Interview with Ministry of the Interior official, Ministry of the Interior, Lima, August 1988.

46. Zileri, "Coca y catástrofe."

47. Before Sendero's success, there was evidence of political work on the part of leftist groups such as MIR-IV (Movimiento de Izquierda Revolucionaria-Cuarta Etapa) that later would join MRTA, PUM (Partido Unificado Mariatequista), and "Red Fatherland" in the Huallaga Valley area. Gonzáles, "Coca y subversión en el Huallaga," 67–68.

48. Ibid., 70.

49. Ibid., 71.

50. See also, "Sendero en el Alto Huallaga, encuentro," Caretas (September 7, 1987): 34.

51. See Cohen, "Cocaine Rebellion." Estimates are placed as high as 10 percent of the output. Raúl Gonzáles gives the sum of U.S. $30 million, which represents 5 percent of his working data (his data are quite different from the data used in this volume). Gonzáles, "Coca y subversión en el Huallaga," 72.

52. Gonzáles, "Coca y subversión en el Huallaga," 70.

53. Because Peru's foreign exchange earnings from traditional exports continue to decline, entrepreneurs in Lima and other commercial centers must rely increasingly on narcodollars available in the black market (referred to as "Ocoña dollars" in Peru) to purchase legitimate imports.

54. Jimmy Torres, "Aucayacu: Territorio de combate," Caretas (November 28, 1988): 39.

55. Gustavo Gorriti, "Sendero en la selva," Caretas (May 7, 1984): 12.

56. "Alianza de narcotraficantes y terroristas: ¡Toman Tocache!" 76–85.

57. Raúl Gonzáles, "El Huallaga, un año después: El retorno de lo reprimido," Quehacer 54 (August–September 1988): 42–44.

58. Gonzáles, "El Huallaga, un año después," 42. Similar accounts abound in other Peruvian journals.

59. Many of the slogans mentioned here were taken from Zileri, "Coca y catástrofe," 42–43.

60. The MRTA, a radical Marxist group led by Víctor Polay Campos, emerged in 1983. It is believed that the MRTA is connected with the M-19 revolutionary group in Colombia, with the Sandinistas in Nicaragua, and Cuba.

61. Author's personal notes. Also reported in an interview with Víctor Polay Campos, conducted by Mario Campos, "¡Monte adento!" *Caretas* 982 (November 23, 1987): 17.

62. Testimony of an investigator in the National Attorney's Office, Lima, January 1989.

63. A particularly chilling instance of Sendero's ruthlessness and the government's vulnerability was the attack on the Uchiza police station, March 27, 1989. See "Uchiza: ¡Nunca Más!" *Caretas* 1051 (April 3, 1989): 11–15, 84–85.

64. "La misión de Mariano," *Caretas*, May 28, 1984, p. 17.

65. Ibid.

66. The political and military chief of the operation and 13 other army officials were under military investigation for drug trafficking as of December 1987. José Gonzales, "Se despunta Sendero?" *Debate* 47 (November–December 1987): 36.

67. See "Tocache y Uchiza eran 'tierra de nadie,'" *Expreso*, July 19, 1987, p. 10.

68. Peruvian Panamericana Television aired an extensive special report (on the *Panorama* series) on the activities of the MRTA in the Upper Huallaga in early November 1987. *Caretas* also had special reports about the MRTA in vol. 980 (November 9, 1987), and 982 (November 23, 1987).

69. Gonzáles, "El Huallaga, un año después," 45.

70. Interview with Ministry of the Interior official, Ministry of the Interior, Lima, August 1988.

71. Individuals within these services – not the forces per se – are the ones susceptible to corruption by drug money. An incident particularly illustrative of interservice rivalries took place in Palo de Acero in July 1988. An army captain attempted to halt a police raid under way in a cocaine-paste production lab. Although strong threats were exchanged, the police ultimately prevailed. U.S. $423,000 in cash was seized, and eight people were arrested, who are undergoing prosecution in the province of Leoncio Prado, department of Huánuco. Information obtained from an official at the National Attorney's Office.

72. Technically, a state of emergency would replace civilian rule with military rule. But in these cases both military and judicial rule coexist in the same territories, with a resulting confusion of jurisdictions.

73. "Arciniega: Yo acuso," *Caretas* 1082 (November 6, 1989): 38–39, 72.

Chapter 7

1. The Peruvian National Jury of Elections confirmed data released by the media: 46 mayors have been assassinated; the governing bodies in 179 municipalities are not operating and in 101 municipalities have been officially closed; and 352 council members from various municipalities are absent from meetings. See Carlos Tovar, "La estrategia del miedo, Las elecciones en peligro?" *Expreso* (Lima), June 28, 1989, p. 10, and "Presidente del Jurado Nacional de Elecciones confirma: Más de 80 distritos sin autoridades municipales," *Expreso*, June 29, 1989, p. 7.

2. Violence is the chief problem in Peru today. In a recent survey, 92 percent of the Peruvian population expressed fear that the country is falling under patterns of violence, with terrorism cited as the principal cause. *El Comercio* (Lima), June 8, 1989, p. A-4.

3. See "Sendero Luminoso internacionaliza la guerra popular," *Oiga* (December 12, 1988): 19, and "Embajada protesta por detenciones arbitrarias," *Expreso* (Lima), June 10, 1989, p. 12.

4. For further information, see "Sendero habría realizado cita cumbre en Argentina," *Expreso*, April 18, 1989, p. 8 (AFP News Agency).

5. Ibid.

6. Pedro Planas, "El Perú está al borde del abismo," interview with Army General Sinesio Jarama, *Oiga* 413 (January 9, 1989): 22.

7. Ibid., 21.

8. Economists call it hyperinflation. Peru's accumulated inflation from March 1988 to March 1989 was 3,208 percent. Instituto Nacional de Estadística, *Informe Económico* (March 1989): 136.

9. Ministry of Interior, interview with a high official, August 1988.

10. Fujimori and Vargas Llosa had the highest percentages of votes in Ayacucho, Apurímac, Huancavelica, Huánuco, San Martín, and Junín. *Expreso*, April 18, 1990, p. 3 (table).

Index